THE
Living Wreath

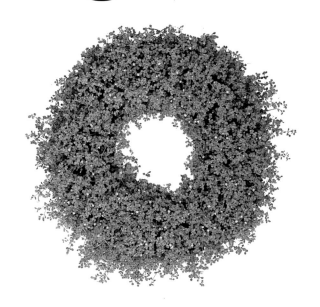

THE Living Wreath

BY TEDDY COLBERT

PRINCIPAL PHOTOGRAPHER
CHAD SLATTERY

GIBBS·SMITH PUBLISHER

SALT LAKE CITY

03 02 01 00 7 6 5 4 3

Published by
Gibbs Smith, Publisher
P.O. Box 667
Layton, UT 84041

Design and composition by Lezlie Sokolik
Edited by Caroll Shreeve
Printed in China

Library of Congress Cataloging-in-Publication Data

Colbert, Teddy
The living wreath / by Teddy Colbert ; principal photographer, Chad Slattery
p. cm.
"A Peregrine Smith book"—T.p. verso
Includes bibliographical references (p.125) and index
ISBN 0-87905-700-9
1. Wreaths. 2. Gardens, Miniature. I. Slattery, Chad, 1947- . II. Title
SB449.5.W74c64 1996
635.9'86—dc20   95-42169
                    CIP

The Living Wreath has the magic
of a garden and the excitement of a master-
piece within a timeless art form.

*To my husband, Ed, our children,
and their families.*

CONTENTS

FOREWORD

by Robert Smaus, *Los Angeles Times* garden editor

I can't explain why the circular shape of a wreath is so satisfying, but nothing looks better centered on a front door or hanging above a hearth. A favorite place of mine is on my garden gate, a rusted relic made by the Stewart Iron Works of Cincinnati around the turn of the century. The only trouble is, unlike my garden gate, wreaths don't last. Even wreaths of dried materials soon get dusty (and really don't take to a hosing off).

Back in November of 1977, an avid gardener and writer named Teddy Colbert came up with a story idea for the *Los Angeles Times* that was more than a new wrinkle in wreaths. It was a whole new way of making this very old and traditional decoration—she proposed building Christmas wreaths of living succulents using little sedums, crassulas, echevarias, and others.

For readers of the *Times*, it was a natural. Traditional holiday wreaths had no staying power. Drying Santa Ana winds, so typical in Southern California around the holidays, shriveled even the toughest balsam wreath mail-ordered from Maine. They might still smell wonderful on Christmas day, but after three or more days of strong winds that can bring the humidity below 10 percent, traditional wreaths look tired and brown, especially on a front door that faces into the low winter sun.

Succulents were another story. Facing the sun is their forte, and dry winds don't faze them at all. Everybody knows succulents can live for years, even suspended well above the ground on a front door. Are they as appealing as the normal cut greens? I'll say! Succulents can be very colorful, certainly a match for the greens and grays of evergreens, or even the reds and oranges found in winter berries, and what they might lack in fragrance, they make up for in form and texture. It was such a natural idea, and it didn't take much of a leap to realize that a succulent wreath could hang on the front door for most of the year, warmly welcoming visitors in any season.

To make it work, Teddy invented a wreath form that would hold a little bit of soil, more than enough for most succulents, and then went on to use these wreaths indoors as well as out, hanging them on interior walls or over the hearth, or laying them flat on their sides with candles in the middle, then later in a model with hidden candleholders right in the frame. Once they came indoors, anyone could make one, no matter where they lived, and while succulents can take just about all the sun you can throw at them, they are also remarkably good at doing without, at least for a while.

They were an instant hit with our readers, even with those ex-Angelenos living on the other coast who still subscribed to the *Times*. But the materials for these wreaths were a little hard to find back then, so a few years later, Teddy started her own company to provide the metal forms and batches of mixed succulent cuttings. Through the years, she has refined the construction methods, discovered all sorts of new candidates for planting in wreaths—even alfalfa sprouts and designer lettuce—and developed more than a few new ways to use a wreath. She's kept her wreaths completely up to date, using brand new plants such as the exciting 'Purple Wave' petunias, which seemed designed for wreaths.

All these innovations finally outgrew the little booklet she had published on making living wreaths so it was only a matter of time before this book had to appear. As I said, it was a natural idea.

PREFACE
by Teddy Colbert

When, after thirty years, it came time to leave our family home in Brentwood, I mentally kicked, fussed, and growled. But like the propagated crassulas, sedums, echevarias, and other succulents in my living wreaths, I am so happy in our new Ventura County home in Somis that, a bit shamefacedly, I realize I was born to live here.

The uncanny ability of succulent cuttings to make a new start after being severed from their life support became an ultimate metaphor as well as the key to the construction of the now-classic, living succulent wreath presented in Part One and that of other living wreaths presented in Part Two.

That phenomenon of the succulents was presented to me as part of my garden-writing education by Duane O. Crummett, Ph.D., in his 1976 Container Gardening class at UCLA, where I was a student of horticulture. Our class assignment was to create a plant container, which eventually became the subject of this book.

From the time I had lived in Europe twenty-two years before, I carried an image of wreaths banked with cut evergreens, crowned with four candles— one for each week before Christmas. The wreaths were fresh and lovely for the first several days, but as weeks went by they became more hazardous and less lovely. I thought, although I had never seen one, "Why not create a living wreath and enjoy its freshness and beauty all year around?"

The living succulent wreath, as I conceived and developed it, was born in that classroom under the mentoring and kindly prodding of Dr. Crummett. The wreath flourished as did my career as a garden writer. Editor Carolyn Murray and garden editor Dan McMasters of the *Los Angeles Times* asked me to contribute to *Home Magazine*. The living succulent wreath and its construction technique made their debut in that publication in November 1977, *Woman's Day* featured it in 1980. The improvised frames of my original wreath corroded but not my determination to improve them; a voice whispered "go on." A new wreath development utilized a more substantial wreath frame of galvanized steel and most of the original succulents.

I continued to make living wreaths for family and friends but was not aware of their potential until a priest friend, Father Sylvester Ryan, now Bishop of Monterey, requested a living advent wreath for his new majestically proportioned church in Tujunga. He urged me to "think big." The parishioners and I constructed a wreath that approached four feet in diameter. Fifteen years later, it is still used in their liturgy. (See the photo on page 73 illustrating Great Group Activity.)

The wreath constructed in 1984 on the more durable frame was photographed for the 1989 *Los Angeles Times Garden Calendar*. Editor Angela Rinaldi suggested that I consider building a business around it. I took her advice.

Both that living wreath, now approaching its twelfth year, and my business are flourishing at this writing. Approximately 14,000 "Living Succulent Wreath" instruction booklets have been sold from Stockholm to Singapore and Alaska to Argentina. The media responded and credibility acknowledged my work through features in *Home, Harrowsmith, The Cactus and Succulent Journal of America, Country Living, House Beautiful, Sunset, Better Homes and Gardens,* and *Horticulture,* as well as numerous regional publications.

My garden-writing career began in 1975 on the crest of the "green revolution," a wave of great national interest in plant life. The criteria seemed to be measured by the number of houseplants an indoor gardener could fit in a room. Home owners in greater numbers were digging up their lawns to plant vegetables. While the momentum of gardening remained over the next decade, the average size of our nation's home gardens continued to shrink. A discernment and creativity began to evidence itself as home gardeners tried to make their limited garden space more satisfying. Interest in specialty produce rather than staple vegetables changed the food market, and innovative topiary increased. The living succulent wreath that held hundreds of rooted plants in an artful form seemed made for its time.

In 1991, organizers of the National Topiary Conference, cosponsored by The National Ivy Society and The San Diego Zoo, invited me to participate with thirteen other artists. They recognized the living wreath as a new topiary art form. The following year, one of my living succulent wreaths "introduced" me to Martha Stewart, who is, like myself, an unabashedly passionate gardener and now a stalwart friend. Martha, as she explained to her television viewers, was visiting a garden of designer Nancy Goslee Powers in Southern California, when she saw one of my succulent wreaths on the garden wall. With a spontaneity and incredulousness that the wreaths seem to evoke, she exclaimed, "*What* is that?"

Martha carried her enthusiasm for the living wreath to her readers in *Martha Stewart Living* magazine's May 1992 issue, in June to her viewers on *The Today Show*, and in a segment on her own syndicated television series in 1993 that has been repeated several times.

That introduction gave me a new insight into gardening in America.

An amazing 90 percent or more of my customers have been roll-your-sleeves-up-and-do-it-yourself gardeners, regardless of their economic status. They are a part of a national renaissance of unprecedented, creative homemaking that has been elevated to an art form. There is no doubt in my mind that Martha Stewart is the sustaining source of that inspiration for countless men and women, helping them experience a satisfaction and transcendent insight as they create beauty where there was none before.

It was no surprise to me when Edward Kasner, Editor in Chief of *Esquire* magazine, in a July 1995 interview on *The Today Show*, listed her as one of the ten most loved women in the world, and in his opinion, one of the ten most influential.

Kindled by the creative energies I encountered and a new ability to "think big," I expanded the concept of the living wreath to a new dimension. The unique living wreaths of flowers, herbs, fruits, and ornamentals that resulted are presented in Part Two of this book.

There are times when I look at my lovely large garden and see the provoking wood stub on the apple tree, overlooked during pruning in the dormant season, or dejected iris flowers begging to be clipped and to start their metamorphosis in the compost bin. I plead with them, "Do not overwhelm me!"

On the other hand, my living wreaths seem to beckon, "Come play with me."

PHOTO BY BILL ROSS

No two wreaths are alike, yet they are all beautiful. Each reflects the character and ability of an individual—romantic, vivacious, formal, or gentle—and conveys the refreshing uniqueness inherent in each of us.

ACKNOWLEDGEMENTS

The living wreath is the flowering of one idea rooted in the soil of family enthusiasm for the earth, richly amended by great teachers, generous colleagues, supportive friends and helpful staff, and constantly nourished by my family.

No words I write can be adequate to thank them. Most of all, my appreciation is to my husband, Ed, who saw this book within me long before I did and whose constant support brought it to fruition.

My Uncle Lawrence Huschle, a landscape architect, first brought me his vision of created beauty in nature when I was a little girl. Uncle Larry's story is told in "Spinach Wreaths and Rose Bushes" in Part Two. To my father, Joe Huschle, who saw that I always had a garden patch for my cosmos, carrots, and black-seeded Simpson lettuce, and my mother Mae who received my crops with more enthusiasm than perhaps they really warranted.

Ron Funk, a friend and former neighbor, as managing editor of the *Santa Monica Evening Outlook* first offered me a position as garden writer. The timing was fortuitous; the last of our seven children had just entered school. So did I, and eagerly began studies of journalism and horticulture.

At the *Outlook,* my first editor was Bill Beebe, who has remained a friend in spite of his honing of my beginning garden-writer work. Then Bill's assignment for me to cover a story on Duane O. Crummett, Ph.D., professor of horticulture at UCLA veered my life in another direction that is constantly presenting other horizons to explore. The wealth of horticultural knowledge and materials that Dr. Crummett exposed me to was one treasure, his leadership was another. He literally placed me into the hands of the garden editor of the *Los Angeles Times* by asking me to write an announcement describing his new classes and insisting I deliver it. My awe was dispelled by the kindly reception from Dan McMasters, who led me by the hand that day to meet Carolyn Murray, the editor in chief of *Home Magazine.* Over the following years, until her early retirement from the magazine, I felt privileged to contribute to her legendary work that beat with the creative pulse of Los Angeles.

Bob Smaus, became the new garden editor after Dan McMasters retired. His teamwork helped build garden-writing epics, in spite of diminishing editorial resources. I am pleased and grateful for his responsive acceptance to write the foreword of this book.

There is a precious and vital unsung corps of assistants whom all writers value: librarians. In files and volumes, seemingly unknown to other humans, they produce hidden and precious information that brings another dimension to a researcher's work. My indebtedness extends to Rennie Day, now retired from the children's division of the Los Angeles Library, and Joan de Fato, botanical librarian at the Arboretum of Los Angeles County and plant sleuth extraordinaire. I am in great debt to the botanists across the country who opened their resources, hearts, minds, and homes, and who shared their wondrous plants, some from their private gardens. My deep gratitude goes to the late Mildred Matthias, Ph.D., a friend and mentor who shared my vision of making the world a better and more beautiful place and joined with me to bolster Gardens for Kids,Inc., a children's gardening education foundation. I am also indebted to the Huntington Botanical Gardens in San Moreno, California, and their curators, John Trager and Joe Clements, who shared experimental plant material and an education beyond that of books, and gave patient response to my intrepid questions.

Friends and family who are so close to me are the hardest to thank. But Carolyn Koegler, my friend who pioneered with me through baby and child raising, through Dr. Crummett's class, and through my initial treks to the San Francisco Landscape Garden Show to introduce my wreaths, has my loving thanks. Nancy and Bob Andersen are treasured friends who initially sponsored me at that show. They not only house me, supply missing work aprons and last-minute moss replacements but welcome me with supreme hospitality at what has become a yearly highlight.

I am indebted to my youngest daughter, Teddy, whose vitality and enthusiasm for the wreaths is contagious. Her assistance at the San Francisco show, pitching in as emergency photographer, and encouragement throughout the year is precious to me.

To other members of my family who have abundantly lent me their expertise—Paul, who designed a data base and guided my frightened entry into the computer world, and Karen, his wife, who whipped data into my new electronic memory and helped me utilize its wonders—I give my loving thanks.

Thanks to my son Tom, whose experience in his news-related IR&D company has been a beacon to me in the uncharted waters of business and book writing; I also appreciate his referral to attorney Bill Jacobson, whose counsel I value. Tom's wife, Dawna Kay, receives my special appreciation not only for her accounting skills that apprise me of the degree of solvency we are in but for emergency computer instructions, trips to the electronic services with our machines for untimely "intensive care," and her general calm in the face of the many "hurricanes" that seem to pass through my life. An accountant and daughter-in-law officially; a friend in reality.

I also thank my niece Claire Huschle, a medieval art historian, for opening a new dimension to me by her research on the symbolism and history of wreaths.

To the rest of my children—Chris, Beth, Peter, and Jeanine—and their spouses, who bravely took Mother's wreaths to campus, and homes, and different environments, and helped my grandchildren understand why they had a little less of "Oma" to play with and that she intends to make up for visits missed during the preparation of this book—I give eternal thanks.

To Gibbs Smith, whose invitation to publish this book has offered a degree of permanence for concepts that hopefully will continue to enhance the lives of future generations as they have mine and those with whom I have been privileged to share them, I am deeply grateful. My appreciation is extended to Caroll Shreeve, my editor at Gibbs Smith, Publisher, for keeping a steady hand on the rudder and for her encouraging and unswerving faith in me and this book.

PART ONE

LIVING WREATH
BASICS

Teddy's "debut" living wreath
hangs on the door of Claire and
Bill Vaughn's home.
PHOTO BY DICK SHARPE

13

In 1984, most of the plants from the original 1977 wreath were transplanted into a sturdier, rust-resistant frame. Twelve years later, as we go to press with this book, the same plants continue to grow in company with newer specimens.

CHAPTER ONE

THE LIVING
SUCCULENT
WREATH

PHOTO BY CHAD SLATTERY

15

INTRODUCTION

The newly rooted succulents look more beautiful than ever, and I am in constant awe at their ability not only to survive but to look better under stress. Their color heightens and their form tends to remain compact when water is minimal and temperatures approach intolerable limits. I ask myself, "Can I ever match that performance?"

Because all of the more recent types of living wreaths I have created are modifications of the living succulent wreath, the basics of that original construction are presented here in Part One, and the modifications that support living floral, edible, and ornamental wreaths are included in Part Two.

ANCIENT HISTORY

The creation of a living wreath is an entry into a new gardening art that embodies ancient and powerful symbolism. Head wreaths were used as early as the time of Moses when Jewish high priests wore wreaths of henbane around their mitres. The implication of using this potent plant, all parts of which are lethal, is unknown to me, but later, the symbolism of the chaplet or head wreath takes a more delightful romantic turn in the spirited writings of Pliny the Elder.

Pliny, a Roman naturalist of the first century A.D., told the tale of a painter named Pausias who fell in love with Glycera, a garland maker in 380 B.C. Pausius included her wreaths in his painting, but wily Glycera kept varying the flowers so that Pausias had to keep returning to paint them accurately. Sixteenth-century painter Peter Paul Rubens recreated the power of that legendary love and the wreaths in his famous *Pausias and Glycera.*

In ancient Greece, lovers hung wreaths on their doorways to show their acceptance of each other. A hazel wreath meant rejection, but if the lady chose an ivy wreath, the suitor could rejoice in his acceptance.

Romans used wreaths of laurel, oak, and myrtle symbolically as head crowns to salute their military victors and athletes. Wreaths of ivy were worn when they feasted to protect them from the effects of too much wine and were then mixed with roses for "secrecy" on occasions when the ivy wreaths were apparently ineffective. From that custom we derive the admonition to confidence; *sub rosa,* or "under the rose," is like the finger pressed to the lips that say, "Hush . . ." Shrines of family gods were decorated with wreaths. They were largely associated with nobility until the revival of private gardening in the late Middle Ages. At that time the home garden gave the less wealthy people access to plant materials that enabled them to craft garlands and wreaths more frequently.

Since only their future husbands could view their uncovered heads, medieval girls wore their hair unbound with a head wreath called a chaplet. Young men as well joined in the practice, and in France, youths wore wreath crowns of leaves for festivals. The custom became common in other European countries such as Czechoslovakia, Hungary, Poland, and Denmark on religious feasts and harvest festivals where the wreaths utilized flowers, grains, and other available plant materials.

Wreaths were used as religious expressions of piety in the shapes of a rosary. The roasted Christmas boar received a head wreath, a custom that was revived later in Victorian England.

The Renaissance saw a heightened interest in the early Roman and Greek culture called the "antique period," and wreaths were incorporated into family emblems and decorations such as the laurel wreath Lorenzo di Medici used in his impresa, or emblem. At an elaborate feast to celebrate the wedding of Cammila of Aragon to Constanzo Sforza of Milan, huge wreaths of laurel, pine, boxwood, and fir encircled the family crests and were joined by garlands of the same material.

The famous Florentine sculptor Luca della Robbia created a series of Madonna

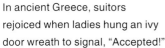
In ancient Greece, suitors rejoiced when ladies hung an ivy door wreath to signal, "Accepted!"

and Child plaques surrounded by sculpted fruit and flowers that bear a striking resemblance to the living succulent wreaths.

It is believed that the European advent wreath began as a Lutheran innovation in the sixteenth century. Its beauty and historical significance triggered my interest and pursuit of a living advent wreath.

Flower painting had reached a highly technical level and esteem in the seventeenth century, and Dutch painters included wreaths on the heads of their madonnas to show off their virtuosity and to increase the value of their work.

THE STORY OF THE LIVING WREATH

In Ulm, Germany, where I taught school before I married, townspeople followed the European Christian tradition of hoisting majestic

advent wreaths with four candles to the rafters of churches and wine stuebels. Homes, classrooms, and shop windows had smaller versions.

The candles were set into the horizontal wreaths, banked with cut fir tree branches, and lit one at a time in anticipation of the birth of the infant Jesus. It was the biggest birthday party I had ever witnessed; schoolchildren cheered as each new candle was lit.

The advent wreaths were

glorious, but as the weeks progressed they became less lovely and more hazardous. An idea began to take root: Why should such a lovely thing be so transient? Why not make a living advent wreath, use it all year with white tapers for weddings and anniversaries, pink or blue for birthdays? Suspend it or lay it on the table for special occasions, as a centerpiece for summer outdoor dinners, holiday buffets, or simply as a fresh arrangement to turn a casual supper into a special celebration? It would also be less flammable and therefore much safer.

DR. CRUMMETT'S CLASS

When I enrolled in Dr. Crummett's 1976 Container Gardening Class at UCLA, I had been carrying those images and ideas for more than twenty years. His class assignment was to create an original plant container. My concept was ready and my idea approved, but my preconceived method was all wrong. I remember the dialogue as he asked me:

"How are you going to get a form for your living advent wreath?"

"Crush chicken wire into a circle," I suggested.

"You can do better than that. Chicken wire corrodes too rapidly."

Then Dr. Crummett showed me two concave wreath forms sold by floral supply stores that could be lashed together to form a circular tube.

"What plants are you going to use?"

"Ivy, what else?" I replied.

"You can do better than that. Ivy demands a lot of attention and water."

Then Dr. Crummett introduced me to succulents. Since my life in the temperate climates of New York and Europe had kept me from discovering these frost-tender tropical and subtropical plants, their forms, textures, hues of green and ample color were new wonders. Their ease of propagation was another. I was incredulous; one cutting, dried and calloused, grew into a new and beautiful plant. No root balls to fall apart, no delicate hair roots to handle, and no concern about keeping them from drying out.

"How are you going to give nutriment to the plants?"

"Stuff the frame with moss and give them a dilute solution of balanced fertilizer with every irrigation."

"Too much trouble. You can do better than that."

"Soil, the good stuff of the earth—I'll mix it with the moss and stuff it into the frame."

"You can do better than that." Dr. Crummett continued to prod me.

"Line the two frames with moss and clap them together?"

"You can do better than that—not enough soil, and the visible frames on the outside are ugly."

"Fill the frames with soil, then wrap it with moss?" I felt I was getting somewhere.

"How are you going to keep the moss in place?"

"I'll wind fishing line all around it." Great, I thought, my husband, Ed, fishes, and we have a garage full of old reels.

But from observations of bonsai artists training their miniature trees into windswept, artful forms, Dr. Crummett suggested the malleable copper wire that they utilized.

"Fishing line is impossible to reposition; one cut and the whole section unravels." He added, "Copper behaves."

I needed no further convincing.

Another advantage of copper wire is that it does not corrode like "florist" wire, and there is no danger of its being toxic to the plant since it is placed on the outside of the root zone.

While the wreath shape in a variety of materials has an ancient tradition, the living wreath is the beginning of a new one. With several wreath styles and a wide spectrum of plant materials to choose from, I believe there is a living wreath to suit most lifestyles and climate conditions located in- or out-of-doors. Although the living succulent wreath can be used for the holidays, it is not a Christmas wreath that goes out with the New Year's trash. It can be used throughout the year—for many years—becoming more of a tradition with each event.

Jack Santino, a professor of popular culture at Bowling Green State University of Ohio, writes of the timelessness of wreaths in his book on holidays. His epilogue reads, "An old folk song asks, 'Will the circle be unbroken, by and by, Lord, by and by?' The circular wreath, a symbol of unbroken time, seems to have joined us as fellow travelers through the year round. . . . Wreaths aren't just for Christmas anymore."

This "Peace on Earth" plaque has a della Robbia-or Brueghel-like, sculptured living succulent wreath for a serene border.

CHAPTER TWO
CONSTRUCTION

PLANNING FOR CONSTRUCTION

Prior to planting, allow approximately one hour to trim and prepare the cuttings. Wait for the cuts to callus over; thick ones take several days. To construct a small living-wreath base and install the prepared succulent cuttings, allow three to four hours for a small size and four to six hours for a large one.

It is easy to make a wreath in stages; the base can be made or purchased ahead and kept indefinitely in dry storage, and then soaked and drained before planting. Thicker cuttings can hold for a week or more. Planting can be done in one area of the wreath at a time.

BASIC HORIZONTAL OR VERTICAL STYLES

The two basic styles for a wreath are vertical and horizontal. The vertical is used on doors, walls, or fences. The larger vertically hung wreaths can be used as frames themselves in the manner of Pieter Brueghel and his sons, Pieter and Jan, the seventeenth-century Flemish artists who excelled in painting flowers and sometimes created frames of them around their artwork.

The horizontal wreaths are used as table wreaths or suspended by hanging chains hooked into their frames. Versatility is increased when custom frames are used with built-in candleholders. Plants camouflage the holders so that both vertical and horizontal wreaths can convert into instant candelabra and return to their original function when the special occasion is over.

Our large custom frames have nine candleholders, but fewer candles may be used as the growing plant material camouflages any unused holders. If a wreath is to be used as a candelabra, I like to use an abundance of light-reflecting plant material such as the silver leaves of *Kalanchoe pumila* shimmering in the candlelight of my neighbor's living-succulent menorah, etched in my memory with their children gathered around the table.

An increasing number of my customers now create suspended living wreaths to use in wedding ceremonies and receptions, and afterwards present them as living and lasting gifts to the bride and groom.

Above: Teddy shares her wreath with Mary Brewer. "We use our suspended succulent wreath before Christmas with traditional advent candles: three purple and one rose. At Christmas I switch to red tapers. For our anniversary we used ivory candles and for our daughter's sweet-sixteen birthday party we chose pale pink tapers." Right: This *Silver Kalanchoe* pumila wreath has served beautifully as a menorah.

20

21

When Can I Make a Wreath?

Wreaths may be created literally any time of the year for an indoor wreath and in the warmer growing season for an outdoor wreath.

Where and How Can a Living Wreath Grow?

A living wreath is a "container plant" and as such can grow anywhere a plant can grow, indoors or outdoors.

Outdoors

Sometimes you can "go around the world" in simulated microclimates on one home property. For the warmest area to grow tropical and subtropical succulents, choose a south-facing, wind-protected location that is elevated, since hot air rises. Cold-hardy succulents prefer a cooler growing area such as a northern exposure that is low in elevation.

Knowing these locations exist can save your living wreaths during severe weather. The sunlight that a wreath receives can vary from full to partial sun with filtered light. I find my twelve-year-old wreath to be very adaptable. Since we moved to our new home three

PHOTO BY CHAD SLATTERY
LOCATION COURTESY OF MARCIA AND DAVID DONLON

Compare the color and texture qualities of two succulent wreaths hung outdoors: one located in full sun and one kept in partial shade.

years ago, it has had three locations with different light exposures: direct western sun, shade of the house, and now it thrives in reflected light. While the colors were most vivid when the wreath grew in strong sunlight, the textures and forms are more noticeable now, and the fresh hues of green convey a welcome serenity.

Indoors

As a rule, I suggest lower-light succulents for growing indoors such as some crassulas, sedums, haworthia, and aeoniums, and recommend a southfacing window or other bright exposure. Supplemental lighting, even a reading lamp in addition to the daylight, is a simple way of keeping the plants vigorous, especially if several days in a row are overcast. Most of my customers in the northern states and Alaska rely on fluorescent bulbs or high-intensity growing lights. Some have a spotlight thrown on a living wreath in their entry as a functional illumination allowing the beauty of the plants to greet arriving guests.

Established plants usually regenerate after pruning. In the case of some crassulas, two shoots should develop where there was one before.

PHOTO BY BILL ROSS

CHAPTER THREE
IT ALL STARTS WITH THE PLANTS

SUCCULENTS

S ucculent tip cuttings
are the essence of a
living succulent
wreath. Not only does judicious cutting pose no threat
to established plants, it most
often leads to a discovery of
the enhancing art of pruning.

Tender succulents must
be protected from below-
freezing temperatures but
many cold-hardy types are
more versatile and can be
included with tender succulents in the wreath: *Sedum
confusum, Sedum
quatemalense, Sempervivum
tectorum* are a few I use most
frequently. The reverse,
however, is not true. For a
wreath to withstand freezing
temperatures, the plant
material must be composed
of all cold-hardy succulents.

To create a wreath, I
group my plants in three categories: background material, accent specimens, and
the smaller-leaved filler
plants.

FAVORITE SUCCULENTS FOR LIVING WREATHS

This is a list of my customers' favorite tender succulents and the ones I most
frequently combine in my
custom wreaths and mail-
order cuttings. Most of them
are tender selections listed
for accuracy by genus,
species, and common names.
Common names can be
ambiguous; for example,
"hen and chickens" in temperate climates means *Sempervivum,* which can live
under the snow and through
freezing temperatures; but in
mild climates it also can
refer to *Echeveria imbricata*
or *Echeveria secunda,* which
do not tolerate freezing temperatures.

Accent Succulents
1. *Kalanchoe fedtschenkoi* 'Variegata'
2. *Crassula corymbulosa* 'Campfire'
3. *Sedum reflexum*
4. *Sedum rubrotinctum* 'Aurora'
5. *Kalanchoe tubiflora* 'Friendship Plant' or 'Chandelier Plant'
6. *Aeonium haworthii* 'Kiwi'
7. *Crassula perforata*
8. *Crassula ovata* 'Baby Jade'
9. *Pachyveria haagei*
10. *Crassula falcata* 'Air plane Plant'
11. *Senecio rowleyanus* 'String of Beads'
12. *Crassula lycopodioides* 'Watch Chain Plant'
13. *Graptopetalum paraquayense* 'Ghost Plant'
14. *Echeveria hybrid*
15. *Sedum Adolphii*
16. *Echeveria hybrid* 'Doris Taylor'
17. *Kalanchoe pumila*
18. *Crassula radicans* (small form)
19. *Crassula radicans* (large form)
20. *Crassula* species
21. *Crassula browneana cf.,* 'Baby's Joy'
22. *Crassula ovata* 'Baby Jade (leaves)
23. *Crassula radicans*
24. *Sedum morganianum* 'Burrito'

Other Popular Plants with Planting Tips
1. Ceropegia: cascading 'String of Hearts,' use as a side drape or for sus-

PHOTO BY VICTORIA PEARSON
COURTESY OF *MARTHA STEWART LIVING* MAGAZINE

pended candelabrum; a romantic addition for a wedding ceremony.

2. Crassula: seem to thrive in any position on a wreath and in sunny or shady locations. They get my award for versatility.

3. Echeveria: prefer a moist soil and are planted in the lower two-thirds of a wreath or just under the top. The large ones make handsome medallions on the face of the wreath, and I like to play up their drama by adding a drape of a few "Donkey Tails" *(Sedum morganianum),* "String of Pearls," or a slender leaf shower of *Othonna capensis* with its dancing, small, yellow, daisylike flowers.

4. Kalanchoe: usually have a linear, upright, growth habit, so they are best flanking the face of the sides.

5. Sedum: generally prefer the drier areas on the top one-third of the wreath, but *Sedum confusum* is an exception and likes moist conditions.

6. *Othonna capensis:* has a Dr. Jekyl and Mr. Hyde dual personality that continues to amaze me. My original stock was an experimental gift from the Huntington Botanical Garden where they use it as a ground cover. When grown in that fashion, juvenile leaves resemble its common name of 'Little Pickles,' but when allowed to trail from a suspended wreath or the side flank of a vertical wreath, they elongate and flow down like Santa's beard.

Background Plant Material

To unify the design, I prefer first to install a single type of plant material on the outside and inside parameters of the wreath base. The result is a wreath-within-a-wreath appearance. The same cuttings are used intermittently between the accent plants. When finished, the total amount of background cuttings is usually equal to the number of accents. (See chart on page 33.)

For tender succulent wreaths, including the lower-light ones, I use cuttings of miniature or dwarf jade (*Crassula ovata* and *C.o.* 'Crosby's Compact'). Standard jade can be used appropriately for large-scale wreaths if that is all that is available (See Great Group Activity on page 74). It will, however, require more vigilant prunings.

For hardy wreaths, I like to mix my background plants using *Sedum spurium* 'Dragon's Blood,' *Sedum acre,* and *Sedum confusum.*

Filler Plants

These diminutive-leaved cuttings are added, not so much to cover the wreath base but to add character. Delay planting these fragile cuttings in the wreath until after the larger cuttings are installed to avoid unnecessary handling. When you receive the cuttings, use a forceps to plant the fillers in pots of moist soil until planting time in the wreath itself.

There are still a few mysteries to the nomenclature of these fillers. Although most of them were given to me by scholars and have been scrutinized by experts, the complete taxonomy remains a secret.

Crassula browneana cf. 'Baby's Joy'—
Our first grandchild was born when I discovered this charming, frothy plant. The constantly blooming, small white flowers and tiny round leaves reminded me of 'Baby's Breath' and 'Baby's Tears,' so the name 'Baby's Joy' seemed appropriate and timely.

'Baby's Joy' is a scandent, or climbing, tender plant that does well in full or part sun and, according to the botanical knowledge available to us, it is a native of India.

Galium verum
'Bedstraw'—
This is a tender, frothy, tufted plant with a taproot. Straight multibranched stems with minute, pointed, opposite leaves of chartreuse green give a bristly texture to the wreath. Its pleasant scent lent its other name, 'Lady's Bedstraw,' referring to the days when people would sleep on a mattress of this and other scented plants. While cuttings are the best way to propagate 'Bedstraw,' any crumbs of the plant that break off seem to root instantly. It welcomes part shade but can handle full sun when established. My original plant came from Jack Catlin's nursery in La Canada, California.

Crassula sarmentosa
'Mildred's Mystery'—
In my experience, this is the most versatile plant I have. It came from the garden of my friend and mentor, the late Mildred Matthias, Ph.D., Professor Emeritus of Botany at UCLA. With a classic understatement, Mildred said, "It grows in the sun or shade; I think it will do well in your wreaths." I have found not only does it do well in any portion of the wreath, both indoors and outdoors, but thrives as well in the blazing sun on our front slope and in the shaded area in the rear. The bright, yellow green leaves shoot out from widely spaced nodes, giving a wreath, in my opinion, an electric "spark."

In 1894, English plantsman, Wilson Saunders, wrote that he thought *Crassula sarmentosa* would take over Kew. Perhaps they pampered theirs more than I do, but mine is very much in control, probably because I have so many requests for cuttings.

HARVESTING THE CUTTINGS

Because a living succulent wreath is based on the uncanny ability of a succulent cutting to thrust out new roots after drying and callousing over, propagation is stunningly simple. With a sharp pruning clipper or garden scissors, take a two- to three-inch tip cutting from branched succulents such as jade or kalanchoes, or sever the top of rosette forms at the same length. If plants such as echeveria and aeonia have already produced "pups" growing along the stem, either snap or cut them off.

Prepare a stub approximately one and one-half inches long by trimming off discolored and bottom leaves. On branched varieties, remove any part of a stem below a node so that the rooting enzymes concentrated there will have better contact with the soil.

Even the trimmed succulent leaves are propagation material. Frugal gardeners (I am one) and children like to watch the tiny root starting to probe the air, looking for a meal. Spread the leaves on a pot of soil, and in time you will have a forest of little plants. Because I live in a mild climate, I have sown jade leaves like seeds on vacant spots in my landscape and now have a border of jade plants around my house.

Vital Drying for Callus Formation

Spread the cuttings in a single layer away from direct sunlight in an area with a lot of air circulation. In my home, a section underneath the family picnic table serves nicely. A perforated plastic nursery tray or shallow basket with another inverted underneath allows maximum air circulation.

If severed echeveria or aeonia are top heavy, a simple way to support them while they are drying—without marring their rosettes—is to insert the stem ends into small terracotta pots whose diameter is slightly smaller than the rosette.

Succulents tend to rot if they are not kept dry. Occasionally, some recipients incorrectly associate them with bare-root plants and moisten the wrapping or put them in water.

SOURCES OF SUCCULENTS
The Garden Landscape

Succulent cuttings can be as accessible as your own

backyard. Although cold-hardy types are limited to the warm growing season in temperate regions, tropicals and substropicals can be found throughout the year in frost-free areas.

For those who have succulents in the landscape, collecting the material for wreaths frequently solves the dilemma of what to do with the prunings.

"Thank heaven," said a customer from the Midwest, "I have barrels of hen and chicks."

Sometimes a well-timed offer of, "May I help you prune your succulents?" is a double benefit.

The Living Succulent Wreath, A Collector's Showcase

At the 1989 San Francisco Landscape and Garden Show, Martin Van Hook, then-president of the Cactus and Succulent Society of San Francisco, saw a six-year-old display model and viewed it as a collector's showcase. Van Hook speculated that the living succulent wreath might bring attention to succulents as a long-overlooked ornamental.

All welcome the new intimacy and eye-level focus to feature their choice specimens in the wreath. In addition to having a showcase, everyone from plant collectors to novice succulent growers has a future supply of plant material as the maturing plants require trimming.

Container Collections

Few outdoor or indoor gardeners of container-grown succulents have the quantity of plant material required to cover a living wreath (See caption for amount of cuttings on page 55). Supplemental or a full supply of cuttings can be obtained from the following additional sources.

The Local Nursery

Generally, the most advantageous purchase from a local nursery can be a flat of ground-cover succulents such as *Sedum quatemalense, Sedum spurium* 'Dragon's Blood,' *Sedum confusum,* and *Sedum acre.* Not only can cuttings from the flats be used immediately, but the trimmed plants can be planted into the landscape to regenerate and provide an

ever-ready supply of fresh wreath materials.

But beware—once you are captivated by succulents, you will not be able to bypass a display at your nursery or anywhere else.

Plant Societies

Check your local botanical gardens, arboretums, and horticultural and garden societies for announcements of succulent shows and plant swaps for the best bargains of rare and unusual plants, and, of course, for enthusiastic camaraderie.

Mail-Order Cuttings

Since mail-order succulent cuttings do not require the packing or have the shipping weight of rooted plants, the cost per cut (each of which is potentially a future plant) is only a fraction of the price of an entire plant. Another advantage of mail-order succulent cuttings is the diversity of specimens offered, customized to the location and personal style of the customer.

Mail-order plant nurseries are listed in Sources at the end of this book.

Care of Mail-Order Cuttings

Unwrap your mail-order cuttings immediately, even if you are unable to trim them right away. The fleshier cuttings such as jade can wait as long as two weeks. However, treat the thin-stemmed plants such as the filler plants 'Baby's Joy,' 'Bedstraw,' and 'Mildred's Mystery' as described on page 28, and insert their trimmed-stem ends into their own pots of moist potting soil until planting time. Since they root very quickly, you may prefer to cut off the top portion and let the roots regenerate as reserve stock, enjoying them as indoor or outdoor container plants.

Having the right tool for each step in creating a living wreath makes the work easier and protects delicate plant cuttings during the insertion process. Clippers, Cushing forceps, or long tweezers, shish kebab sticks, copper wire, and wine corks are among the most essential "helpers" you will need in your assortment of efficient tools.

Chapter Four
The Materials You Will Need

31

MATERIALS AND TOOLS

I feel a little like I imagine God must feel when I survey my plants and living wreaths. With a notebook in my pocket to capture the great thoughts that come to me in my garden, and forceps in my hand, I tug out a sickly yellow leaf, interrupt a munching caterpillar, or plant a young succulent offshoot. After I slap the tool back into my pocket and jot down a few notes, I'm ready to tackle the rest of the day.

TOOLS AND ACCESSORIES

These are listed in order of use with substitutes and quantities where indicated:

1. Plastic drop cloth, two to three sizes larger than the frame being used. A new, unfolded thirty-gallon trash bag is usually the most accessible.
2. Wooden shish kebab sticks (a dozen or two), pencils, or chopsticks.
3. Pliers with wire-cutting edges.
4. Garden scissors or pruning clippers.
5. Forceps with a straight edge, or long tweezers.
6. Latex surgical-type disposable gloves for handling the moss.
7. A few fern pins or large hairpins.
8. # 24 gauge copper wire, spooled or wound on a paddle.

Tools are personal, an extension of ourselves. Consider whether the tools fit your hand, are unwieldy, and if the weight responds to a good heft. One of my favorites for making and grooming my wreaths—in addition to tending to my other plants—is an economical copy of the Cushing dressing forceps, a surgical tool.

Cushing forceps are large tweezers—approximately five to seven inches long—that allow me to slip slender stems such as those of 'Baby's Joy' into the soil core of the wreath base. I can also open a wedge in the wreath base with the flat handle, and the pincers help me to tuck in the delicate hair roots of transplants or to place seeds exactly where I want them.

The principles of horticulture are not always learned in the classroom or from a book. Three years after I originated the living succulent wreath at UCLA, I continued to perfect my technique. The wreaths I made became gifts to friends and family who marveled at their "little gardens." But I was not satisfied. The wreaths were pretty, unique, and remained in good but not great condition. What was missing?

My answer came during a holiday trip to Santa Catalina Island off the coast of Southern California. Although I had learned in botany class that the secret of successful plant culture is to study the nature of a specimen's habitat, I had never "botanized" or traveled with plant sleuths to study locations where plants originated. I finally had the opportunity.

The *Dudleya hasseii*, indigenous to Catalina, was there to greet me as I stepped off the passenger boat. There, on an east-facing cliff near the dock, were the silver starbursts of this Catalina native, living, incredibly enough, in the cracks of the precipitous cliff. The soil around their roots was minimal—the "lean cuisine" of nature; the drainage from sparse rainfall their only source of water, the fresh sea air swirled around the entire plant constantly.

Those craggy silver beauties showed me what I had missed in my research: aeration and drainage. My early wreath technique had not provided for proper consideration of either, but was remedied simply enough by slipping a half frame under or behind the planted wreaths—a principle later incorporated into my custom frame by adding legs or spacers. This allowed "air pruning" to the delicate feeder roots that had previously rotted in the undrained underside of the wreath base. Gardeners such as myself are admittedly a bit madcap, but I still maintain that those rescued succulent wreaths perked up instantly, took a deep gulp of air, and gasped, "At last!"

Plant supply and a wreath's growing condition

limit my use of *Dudleya hasseii*, but, when appropriate, I try to include one in each of my custom wreaths as a tribute to a memorable and instructive experience.

HARDWARE

Wreath Frames

"What size frame shall I buy?" is one of the first questions asked by gardeners buying their first living-wreath frame. To decide, visualize a finished wreath four inches larger than the frame size, allowing more for bouffant plant material such as petunias, spider plant *(Chlorophytum comosum),* and leaf lettuces, and less for more compact growth of ivy, diminutive succulents, and salad sprouts.

Consider durability and versatility when purchasing frames. Improvised frames are lightweight and naturally do not stand up to long periods of moisture in a living wreath. Custom frames are made of heavier galvanized steel to resist corrosion and to support the saturated weight of the wreath without sagging.

Living wreaths can be constructed in three ways:

1. Custom and patented living-wreath frames: These are constructed of #12 gauge galvanized steel (or #10 gauge for the largest 18-inch size) with short "spacers" or legs to ensure essential aeration and drainage. The built-in candleholders will be hidden by the foliage of the plants and allow the wreath to be used interchangeably as an instant, horizontal centerpiece, then returned to its vertical position as a wall or door wreath. A suspended, horizontal candelabrum with cascading plants is another option.

2. Improvised living-wreath frames: By utilizing three floral box-wire frames from floral supply stores, a living wreath form can be constructed by lashing two such frames together with copper wire to form a tube and later slipping the third underneath or behind the completed wreath to promote aeration and drainage. These frames usually have a lighter wire gauge and are painted green.

3. Ready-to-plant wreath bases that have moss-wrapped and soil-filled construction on custom frames: These bases can eliminate as much as one-third of the time required to create a living wreath, and have been the most popular wreath-construction method, in my experience. I recommend them to those who are creating a wreath for the first time as a prototype for future construction.

Custom and patented living-wreath frames

Frame size	Finished wreath	cuttings	Uses
18"	22" - 24"	300	Focal point for large wall or fence, end of path or corridor
18"	22" - 24"	300	Door wreath for large-scale door with low traffic
			Custom with optional nine candleholders
			Menorah or large table centerpiece
14"	18"	200	Average door wreath
			Centerpiece
			Advent wreath, church or home size
12"`	16"	175	Door Wreath, average to narrow
			Small panel
			Small table centerpiece
			Advent wreath, chapel or home size
10"	14"	100	Niche accent
			Small table or desktop accessory

Suspended Horizontal Or Candelabra Wreath Hardware

Omit the hanging wire or jack chain noted on page 36 and purchase a suspended wreath hardware unit or assemble the following components:

> Four 18" hooked chains joined by an "S" hook
> One brass swivel
> Another "S" hook for connecting to overhead support

The swivel facilitates rotation of the wreath during planting and afterward so that the plants will receive equal sunlight and develop evenly.

Copper Wire

The amount of wire required for each wreath is in proportion to the outside diameter of the frame being used. Sufficient spooled wire is provided with each custom frame. For the improvised construction, add an extra 10 feet for small frames or 15 feet for large sizes to form the skeleton of a tube by lashing two of the concave half-frames together in four or six evenly spaced sections.

Since copper wire is usually sold in coils, it is

PHOTO BY DICK SHARPE
LOCATION COURTESY OF
BILL AND CLAIRE VAUGHN

recommended that all the wire be initially rewound onto an empty spool or short length of wooden dowel to prevent kinking.

Wire Wrapping

Frame Diameter	Wire Footage
18"	.80"
14"	.60"
12"	.50"
10"	.40"

Hanging Wire or #12 Gauge Jack Chain

The suggested lengths allow sufficient slack for hanging without being visible above the plant material. Another option is #12 gauge jack chain of stainless steel or brass to prevent corrosion. Attach by prying open the end links and squeezing them closed at the junction of two adjacent crossbars.

Heavy Copper Wire

Frame Diameter	Length of Hanging Wire
18"	.16"
14"	.16"
12"	.14"
10"	.12"

Because of their weight, I prefer to suspend sizable wreaths, constructed on 18-inch frames or larger, from two parallel hanging wires to disperse the load and prevent sagging. Always test the weight-bearing ability of the installed hanging hook or nail prior to use.

In my experience, an early and well-learned lesson occurred on a photography location for the 1977 *Los Angeles Times* feature introducing the living succulent wreath. A carefully groomed and coddled specimen more than 30 inches in diameter was placed on a poorly installed nail. After the ensuing crash, photographer Dick Sharpe and I heaved, pushed, and bent back into its classic circle shape what had suddenly become a huge egg-shaped wreath. I set a new time record in replanting the mass of loosened succulents. Those plucky plants—unlike their designer— sailed through their debut with indomitable aplomb.

Sphagnum Moss

Natural sphagnum moss, the kind most commonly used to build a moss-lined basket, is a living product most often found in the forest. While it carries the refreshing scent of its environment, I have recently learned that it also is an occasional host to a troublesome skin fungus called *Cutaneous Sporotrichosis*. For that reason I recommend wearing a pair of latex surgical gloves for protection when handling moss.

Although natural sphagnum moss is sold by the pound, it is difficult to gauge the exact amount needed since it does not have uniform density. Because of that, it is wise to have a surplus supply for patching thin areas, tucking around plants that may be added later, and of course, replacing the loot taken by any feathered robbers during nesting season.

The following quantities are suggested to wrap each frame in the manner described under Wreath-Base Construction. Each amount allows for a circular mat 2.5 times the outside diameter of the frame and provides extra for repairs:

Moss Quantity

Frame Size	Pounds of Sphagnum Moss
18"	.3-4
14"	.2
12"	.1-2
10"	.1

Soil

Standard potting soil is appropriate even for the succulent wreaths that usually require amendments for drainage, such as pumice, sand or perlite. The design and technique of the custom and improvised frames provide for the essential and often overlooked drainage and aeration in the root zone that container plants crave.

Approximate amounts of potting soil for each size frame:

Soil Quantity

Frame Size	Quantity in Gallons
18"	.2 1/2
14"	.1 1/2
12"	.1
10"	.3/4

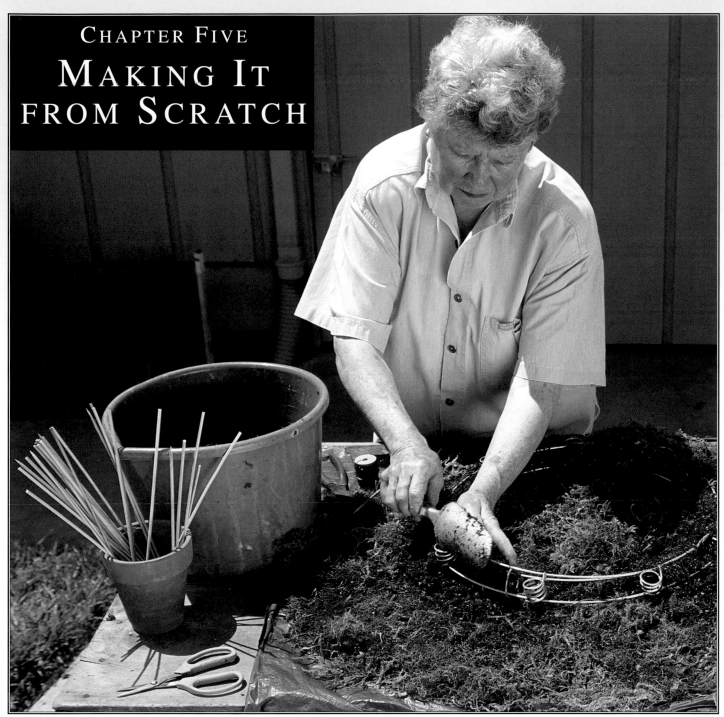

PHOTO BY CHAD SLATTERY

"I WANT TO MAKE IT FROM SCRATCH"

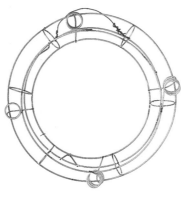

More than 90 percent of my customers who learn about my living wreaths want to make one of their own from scratch. Their response is spontaneous and contagious with a creative urge to gather materials and begin—now!

CONSTRUCTION OF THE LIVING-WREATH BASE

The heart of all the living wreaths is a moss-wrapped frame filled with soil originally designed to sustain the plants in the living succulent wreath. Now with slight modifications explained in Part Two, the new frames and materials are capable of accommodating the needs of appropriate floral, fruit, or ornamental plants.

Teddy Colbert and Martha Stewart on the set of *Martha Stewart Living* TV series during taping of a demonstration of Teddy's living succulent wreath construction techniques for an upcoming segment.

1. Moss preparation:
Soak the quantity of moss needed for your wreath. If it is very dry and surface tension prevents absorption, add one drop per gallon of water penetrant or liquid dish soap to hasten the process. Drain the moss for a few hours or overnight on an elevated screen or a large nursery tray with an inverted one of the same size underneath. Cover the moss with plastic to prevent it from drying out and try to capture the nutrient-rich, drained-off water in a container to irrigate azaleas, gardenias, and other acid-loving plants.

PHOTO BY DON CORREN
COURTESY OF *MARTHA STEWART LIVING* TELEVISION

2. The Work Area:

"Be kind to yourself when setting up a work area," I tell students in my workshops. Very often the excitement to get started makes them over-look simple arrangements that can increase efficiency and prevent back strain.

Select a work area out of the direct sun but with good lighting, and raise the work surface to waist-high level. Cement building blocks, wood blocks, or bricks are usually the most accessible materials. Once you have worked in a waist-level posi-tion, you won't want to revert to a lower-height work surface again.

I learned this convenient suggestion from watching and marveling at the high speed and comfort with which teams in the commer-cial nurseries near my home assemble thousands of trans-plants per hour into color packs for the retail market, singing while they work.

Creating and organizing a work-table that affords comfort over a period of several hours has been perfected by Teddy at a height providing her minimum back strain and maximum efficiency.

PHOTO BY CHAD SLATTERY
'CHIFFON MORN' PETUNIAS COURTESY BODGER SEEDS, LTD.

3. Plastic drop cloth:
Spread a plastic drop cloth or substitute an unused garbage bag to cover your work surface before you begin. Use it to turn the wreath base during construction; cleanup will be easier. Assemble the tools you will need within easy reach to the side of the work area you've created.

4. Form the moss mat:
Pull on your protective latex surgical gloves, then place the moist drained moss in the center of the drop cloth. Turn the more attractive green side or top of the moss down and face the rooted area up since it Wear protective gloves when handling moss. Prepare a plastic-covered surface to construct a mat of moss, root side up, where you will center the framework for the wreath on top, before the soil-wrappng steps.

It is critical that the soil core of the wreath be evenly wrapped with healthy moss. From your "patch pile," add pieces of moss to cover thin spots as you proceed around the wreath base with your wrapping.

will be reversed during the wrapping.

Make a circular mat approximately two and a half times the diameter of the frame. Try to keep sections of the moss intact, and open pieces that have been doubled over in packing.

Add extra moss to thin areas to prevent soil from leaking through, and push all the moss toward the center of the mat. I find it efficient to use my fingers as a measure: to test for an even thickness, poke with your fingers, and check that the moss comes over the first knuckle, approximately 1 1/2 inches deep.

Put a generous supply of moss to the side of your mat for your "patch pile."

5. Placing the wreath frame on the moss:
Put the frame upside down in the middle of the mat with the open end of the candleholders facing down.

If you are making a wreath to be suspended vertically on a door or a wall with a hanging wire, make sure that one end of the wire is securely attached to a crossbar toward the back of the frame arranged to face you on top. Since it is easier to pass the spool of wire around when wrapping the The open ends of the candleholders should be facing down toward your work surface as you wrap the moss around the core of soil in the wreath base. Mark each holder with a shish kebab stick as soil covers it.

44

As the soil covers the crossbar adjacent to the attached hanging wire, a shish kebab stick marks where the open end will be attached. To maintain the air-spaces needed by the roots, do not compact the soil.

base if the end is left open, lay out the other open end perpendicular to the frame. As the wrapping progresses in that section, the open end will be attached to the adjacent crossbar.

6. The core of soil:

With cupped hands, place the moist potting soil over the wire frame so that it fills the inside of the wire structure. To preserve the air spaces that roots need, gently pat the soil but do not over compress and compact it.

Mark the locations of the candleholders and the crossbar adjacent to the attached end of hanging wire by pushing shish

kebab sticks through the mounded soil.

7. Lay moss over the soil:
First, view the moss like a map with four geographical directions, then lift the moss from the outside at north, then south, east, and west points, laying it on the top of the soil core. If the moss is lifted in a continuous circular direction around the mat, a large mass accumulates that can make the base lopsided.

Next, make a hole in the center of the inner circle of moss and gently lift the moss outward and up toward the top. There will not be enough moss to cover, so add Think of the moss base as a map with four compass points. Lifting from the outside at north, then south, east, and west will lend an order to your method of laying the moss on top of the soil core in the base-making process.

Wrapping the moss-covered, soil-filled base with strong copper wire is an important step made easier–and more fun!–with the helping hands of a partner who will enjoy the satisfying results of the finished wreath.

generous patches from your reserve moss supply until all the soil is covered.

8. Coiling the wire:
It is possible to coil wire around the base by yourself, but to save two-thirds of your construction time, find a working partner with a pair of willing hands.

While little skill is demanded for this stage, several spouses who have reluctantly pitched in have been known to brag later about the spectacular living wreaths they helped create.

Open the spooled wire and pass the open end underneath the moss. Lift the moss

PHOTO BY CHAD SLATTERY

slightly so as not to disturb the soil and just high enough to pass the spool under it.

If working with a partner, have your helper hold the moss together with two hands over the section of the wreath base being worked on. After the first pass around, twist the beginning of the wire together with the wire from the spool and pull it taut so that it disappears into the moss. Leave a long tail end of the wire to indicate the beginning of the wrap, and mark where the wire disappears into the moss with a shish kebab stick. Measure the distance to the next interval and continue the process.

Maintain a taut tension on the copper wire as you repeatedly pass it beneath the base. Don't change jobs with a partner or the tension uniformity may be lost. Keep a uniform shape and strength to the wreath overall.

With corks marking the candle holder locations, firmly tug to test the secure attachment of the hanging wire, and give a final check for any thin spots of moss to be patched. Celebrate—the wreath base is ready for planting!

Repeat passing the spooled wire underneath the wreath base. Keeping the same tension on the wire, bring it to the top of the wreath base 3/4 inch away from the stick that marks the first wrap. My forefinger measures a perfect 3/4 inch interval when placed next to a shish kebab stick. You may find that a simple measurement of your own fingers speeds this interval-spacing process. Sticks mark candle-holders for corks or candles.

Move the stick to the side of your finger to mark the new interval and repeat the wrapping procedure all around the soil-filled frame.

9. Wrapping tips:

🌿 Poke a stick through each candleholder to mark its location.

🌿 Make sure the wire does not slip between the coils of the candleholders so that the cavity remains free to hold the base of the candle. As you coil, and your partner shifts hands to a new position, let the your fingers be "eyes" and feel for thin spots of moss or trickles of soil. On discovery of a scantily covered place, patch on moss from your extra pile to repair the problem, even if you have to back up your coiling.

🌿 Protect your back from strain as you progress by rotating the drop cloth to maintain your most comfortable position.

10. Modifying the top section:

If you are constructing a vertical wreath for a door or wall, make sure that the coiling wire does not constrict the attached end of the hanging wire.

The top section of a wreath is where we grapple with the law of gravity. The water given to a hanging wreath is obedient to that

Teddy's patented custom frames and filled bases, available from her mail-order service, are rust-resistant and strong enough to support the weight of a moist, living wreath "miniature garden."

edict and heads for the bottom. There, greedy plants imbibe and later flaunt their herbage to their top-side companions that are impoverished by their short supply of water. To help the upper plants receive a fair share of moisture and to prevent a bottom-heavy wreath, add extra moss to the top area around the hanging wire to retain extra water.

When you reach the stick marking the crossbar adjacent to the attached end of the hanging wire, slip the open end of the hanging wire

through at a right angle to the crossbar. Make sure that the wire does not slip in either direction, and securely attach the wire to that intersection. Test it with a hard tug and adjust if necessary.

11. Ending the wrapping with a flourish:

At the last interval, join the wire on the spool to the "tail" that signals where you began; twist them together several times. Cut off the wire, leaving about three inches. To mark the end with a flourish, form a curl by winding the

wire around a pencil or the end of a pair of forceps.

Hold the base on its side and push the sticks that are marking the candleholders through to the other side, and put recycled wine corks into the candleholders to mark their location and to keep them from filling with soil.

RECYCLED WINE CORKS
My family and friends toast my enterprise and dutifully save their wine corks for my wreaths. Keep corks in the candle cups as you work so that you can incorporate them into the design; then remove them when the planting is finished before they swell with moisture.

COMPLETING THE BASE PREPARATION
Now that you have finished the foundation of your living wreath, congratulate yourself and your partner. You have passed the most challenging phase of creating a living wreath. Do not be discouraged at the time it takes on your first try—it is always the most difficult. With practice, a midsized wreath base with a filled and wrapped frame can be ready for installing the plants in less than 30 minutes.

CHAPTER SIX
THE FUN BEGINS

PHOTO BY DR. DONALD E. BURKE

LOCATION
OF THE LIVING
SUCCULENT
WREATH

Before the succulent plants are installed, the first step to consider is the ultimate location of the wreath and the focus it will receive. As an example, consider the massive, living Christmas wreath I made for my church. The pastor wanted the congregation to enjoy its presentation as they entered the church through open doors, so he had it centered in the curved lintel overhead. I thought the curve of the arch would complement the circular wreath—just like a della Robbia. However, as the wreath was hoisted into position, my strategically placed eye-level accents and sculptural forms emphasizing the crests were obliterated by the abrupt, new focal point. Exposed to baffled viewers below was the unplanted, naked moss bottom of the wreath base. A quick rearrangement taught me always to check the final site and simulate the position during planting as well as to pack an emergency supply of touch-up plant material.

**Vertical-Wreath
Planting Tips:**

🌱 To help keep the focus in perspective as you work, mark the top of a vertical wreath with a shish kebab stick or other marker. Perhaps more important is to hang the wreath periodically during planting—at the future focus level—and, like an artist who steps back from his canvas, view it with fresh eyes.

🌱 For efficiency, locate that position on a wall or fence

Place your living wreath where it will command attention, enhanced by its "eye level" view and dramatic as well as functional night lighting.

near the worktable or use a large "S" hook on a chain-link fence.

Horizontal-Wreath Planting Tips:

A horizontal wreath or candelabrum that is to be suspended usually has a wrap of plant material extending underneath a portion of the outer rim.

🌤 To prevent crushing the plants in that area of the wreath, hang the base at eye level by suspended-wreath hardware containing a swivel to turn the wreath while you work and later to rotate it for equal sunlight. Consult your hardware source for advice on a swivel strong enough to support your saturated wreath.

🌤 Another method of elevating the wreath during planting is to place it on the rim of a nursery can (the five-gallon size fits a base made with a fourteen-inch frame) or a round wastebasket with a diameter the same size as the wreath frame's inside dimension.

🌤 To steady the container while working, weight it down with bricks or stones. It is also a good way to transport a wreath in a vehicle for short distances while having

LOCATION COURTESY OF CLAIRE AND BILL VAUGHN, WREATHS BY WORKSHOP STUDENTS, GLORIA WALLERS AND LISA BANNIES

Insert the calloused stub ends of the plant cuttings up to 300 of them—through the moss wrapping and into the soil core of the wreath base using Cushing forceps, though a pencil or chop stick can make a hole to hold a cutting. Avoid using pins to hold cuttings, by pushing surrounding moss toward the inserted stub; they root faster without compression. Opposite page, note calloused stub end of cutting.

someone other than the driver keep a steadying hand on it, or wedge the can into a packing carton.

INSTALLING THE SUCCULENTS

When I reread my first written instructions for planting a wreath to prepare this book manuscript, I was amazed at my compulsiveness. When developing my first wreaths, I advocated pinning down each inserted stem—200 and 300 of them! Later, I became either wiser or lazy, or a bit of both. After observing the *Dudleya hasseii* living on those precipitous Catalina cliffs, I realized that air around the root zone—not compression and compacting—was what succulents needed. I eliminated the pins. However, I did improve my method of inserting the succulents to give them more traction or holding power within the wreath base.

Installation Technique

With forceps, a pencil, or a chopstick used like a dibble, make a hole through the moss into the core of the wreath-base soil. Insert the stub end of the cutting into the hole as deeply as

possible. Forceps are preferable if the stem is delicate. Insert the forceps parallel to the stub, and push the surrounding moss and soil toward the stem while holding the opposite side rigid with a finger tip. Repeat the procedure on the adjacent side of the stem so that it has good contact from a north, south, east, and west direction. Give it a "tug test" and if it slips out easily, repeat the insertion procedure in another location.

Background Planting

Place the wreath base face down with the candleholders on the bottom. The least accessible inner and outer curved sides are easier to plant from this angle. Start the first closely planted row just beyond the midsection of the inside curve of the base toward the front. As you probe with your instrument, you will feel a heavy support wire that divides the halves of the frame.

Continue around the entire curve and then make a second row, staggering the cuttings in between those of

The insertion of cuttings on the inside curve is more accessible from the back of the wreath base.

PHOTO BY CHAD SLATTERY
PUBLISHED IN *HORTICULTURE*

the first row. Repeat the procedure around the outside curve. The base will resemble a wreath upon a wreath.

Accent Planting

Some floral designers have a formula for focal points of arrangements, but since the wreath is composed of living plants, I respectfully allow the plants to influence their placement in the design. Like the art of landscaping, we look beyond the immediate shape and color of the plantings and consider their growth pattern and cultural needs.

No two wreaths are alike, yet all are beautiful. Each reflects the character and ability of the individual wreath maker—romantic, vivacious, formal, gentle, or bold—and conveys the refreshing uniqueness in us all.

Design Tips:

🌿 Wreath design is a very personal and reflective expression and does not seem

There are 13 species of Rhipsalis in this flamboyant candelabrum. A wreath base is a natural home for this epiphytic cactus. Current location is at the Huntington Botanical Gardens, San Moreno, California.

confined to artistic ability. I have yet to see a well-made wreath that is not pleasing. The following tips may help the novice wreath maker:

🌿 Group the smaller plants as they grow in nature, tucking them under a larger specimen in clusters or fanning out around it.

🌿 Be brave—the more I experiment, the more I make discoveries, such as the wild "bad-hair day" look of little aloes or 'Mildred's Mystery' all around the parameter.

🌿 Do not corral the plants in rows. I have seen some arrangements that resemble bull's-eye targets. Healthy growing plants, even with heavy pruning, soon defy those boundaries.

Special Planting Techniques

To hold a heavy cutting or a shallow-rooted plant such as Haworthia in place, my workshop crew at a Veteran's Hospital helped devise the "voodoo" technque: slip a shish kebab stick under the bottom leaf adjacent to the stem and all the way through the wreath base as a helping hand, then repeat as needed with enough other sticks around

flesh of the stem or leaf, but rather, position the pin to straddle that section.

🐾 Do not trust your fingers to give it a precise touch, but use the rubber eraser of a pencil to push it into place.

🐾 Because it has brittle leaves, plant "Donkey Tail" *(Sedum morganianum)* last. Lay the calloused or dried cutting in the palm of your hand and ease the stem into a hole below the moss and parallel to the surface. To help it remain in that position, secure it with a fern pin or large hairpin that straddles the stem below the moss surface.

Horizontal and Candelabra Wreath Tips:

🐾 Use low-mounding plants such as Echevaria, Haworthia, and 'Bedstraw' on the top surface and sides of the wreath. In suspended wreaths, install cascading succulents such as 'Donkey Tail,' 'String of Hearts,' 'String of Pearls,' 'Mildred's Mystery,' and *Othonna capensis* on the outer sides.

🐾 Protect candelabra plants from dripping wax with a small, flat, doughnut-shaped bobeche of glass, or cut a similar disk shape out of a foil pie plate.

For "special effects," such as the side drape appearance of this wreath, insert the delicate trailing plants last in the planting process. They will eventually become a dramatic flowing beard or a fancy drape.

the plant to support the weight. To remove that look of "witchery" but keep the support, clip off the outside ends of the sticks to just underneath the leaves. After the roots develop and anchor the plant, slip the sticks out with forceps.

🐾 Add delicate plants such as the fillers 'Baby's Joy' and 'Bedstraw' as final touches to avoid their being damaged.

🐾 Occasionally a fern pin or large hairpin is needed to secure a short-stemmed, heavy, or bottom cutting. Never stick the pin into the

PHOTO BY CHAD SLATTERY

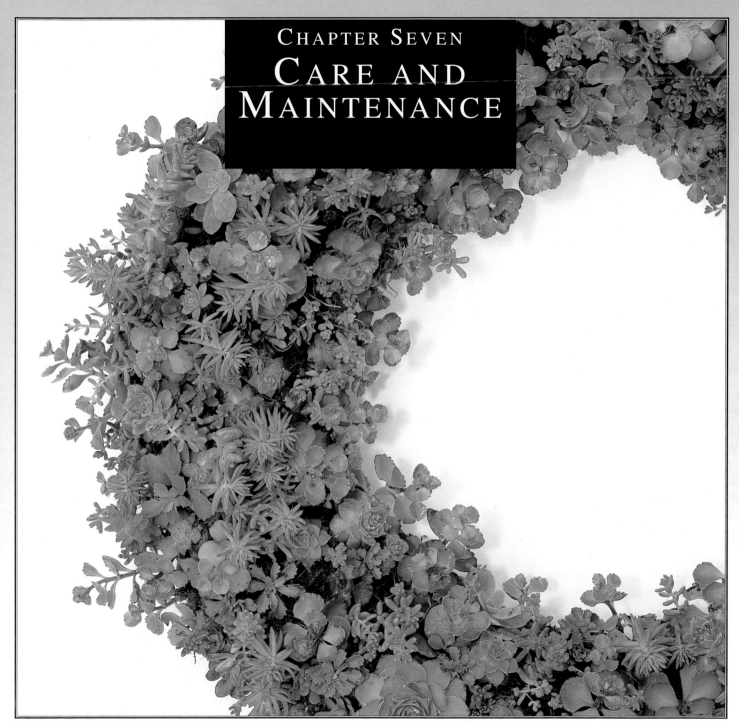

CHAPTER SEVEN
CARE AND MAINTENANCE

THE CARE OF NEWLY PLANTED WREATHS

HANGING THE NEW WREATH

When my technique of installing cuttings as described on page 55 is followed, customers marvel that newly planted wreaths made with my technique can be hung immediately. Generally I recommend a recovery period in a horizontal position to help the roots take hold, but I frequently succumb to the impulse of displaying my work right away. If that is also your inclination, a few topiary pins holding the underside cuttings will keep them from jostling loose.

SUN PROTECTION

More caution is needed for new wreaths' exposure to sunlight. Treat your new outdoor tender or cold-hardy succulent wreath as if you were taking your first dose of sun after being indoors during the winter. Keep it in bright light, out of direct sunlight for one week and gradually introduce it to full exposure. Even then in desert or torrid climates, partial shade from the midday sun is advised.

COLD PROTECTION

Protect all tender wreaths from freezing temperatures. Cold-hardy wreaths need six to eight weeks to be established before they can withstand temperatures to approximately 28 degrees Fahrenheit. (See Care and Maintenance on page 115 for wreaths in temperate zones.)

LIGHT

Outdoors

High light is generally a requirement for the healthy growth of succulent wreaths with protection from midday sun in intense heat for tender as well as for the cold-hardy group. Variations exist depending on the climate and the type of succulents.

PHOTO BY TEDDY COLBERT

Indoors

The same high-light needs exist for indoor succulent wreaths. Lower-light succulents are easier to grow indoors with supplemental lighting on dark days.

Rotation

All horizontal wreaths should be turned regularly to ensure uniform growth. Turn the suspended wreaths by giving a twist to the swivel connected to the drop chain. Tabletop styles should periodically receive a quarter turn.

It's easy to forget this simple rule. Pat Koons received a Mother's Day gift of a lower-light wreath from her daughter Deborah and son-in-law, the late Jerry Garcia. Pat forgot to rotate the tabletop wreath gift, leaving one side unexposed to light. Replacement plants restored the wreath to its original uniformity and Southwest character chosen by Deborah.

Treat your newly planted wreath like a newborn, such as this one with double-planted sides. Shield it from extremes of light and temperature until the roots have formed and the plants are acclimated to their new home.

IRRIGATION

Dunk, Dribble or Drip. "When do I water?" is the most common wreath-care question I receive. My answer is the "loaf-of-fresh-bread-test." Squeeze the wreath from the back; if the moss is dry on the outside but soft inside—similar to fresh bread—do not water. If the moss is dry but beginning to be firm, water the wreath deeply to encourage the roots to go into the core of wreath-base soil.

Never mist or sprinkle with water, very few plants benefit from this since salts build up on the leaves and the roots head for the surface only to be burnt off by the sun. Most succulents are drought tolerant and are accustomed to long periods between watering.

Overwatering or misting are not tolerated by succulents in particular and by most other plants in general. Succulents thrive on what often seems to be minimal water and lots of air. Periodically rotate your indoor wreath a quarter turn so that its foliage flourishes uniformly all around the wreath base in window light .

Dunk

The quick and efficient method of dunking is especially useful for smaller wreaths that are easy to lift. Submerge the wreath in a slightly larger container than the wreath's full size until the bubbles that escape cease coming to the surface. Drain immediately.

If the submerging container is not deep enough, let the wreath sit in the shallow water until it soaks enough water to saturate its moss/soil base, adding water if necessary. Some alternative containers are the tops of circular trash cans, a plugged shower floor, or even a carton lined inside with heavy plastic. When I display my wreaths in shows and cannot pack large containers, this improvised carton and plastic method is a godsend.

One method I use when I am in a hurry, and invariably I am, is to water the top of the wreath, standing it on its topside against the side of the container and then hanging it, allowing the saturated top-portion's water to trickle down and moisten the lower half.

Dribble

A slow dribble from the hose outdoors, where water run-off is not a problem, is an effective wreath-watering procedure, provided that it is done at a slow rate and with repeated applications. Trickle or spray a stream of water over the top of the wreath, then go on to another garden chore. Repeat the procedure until the top portion is saturated. Allow gravity to carry the water to the lower portion.

Drip

Drip irrigation is the most efficient and economical system for watering a living wreath and is especially appreciated by those who live in drought areas.

If a master drip system is already installed, hook up two emitters, one to either side of the crest of the wreath, so that both sides can be watered simultaneously.

For those who do not have a master system or prefer a system independent of the main water pressure line, I offer two plastic bags that each have a thumb-turned control. The drip rate is easily regulated to release water

For wreaths that are heavy, located in awkward-to-reach places, and for gardeners who have difficulty lifting, Teddy re-recommends drip irrigation as an alternative to dunking and dribbling the water and nutriments to the growing plants. Bags are available from her by mail order.

over a few hours, overnight, over the weekend, or during a short vacation. These adapted medical devices are for temporary display and store easily in a drawer or cabinet until the next application is required.

The drip bags can also be used for other hanging plants such as ferns, ivy, and pothos. Bonsai gardeners call them liberating. Drip bags are also ideal for applications of liquid fertilizer and systemic pesticides.

Suggested Rates for Drip Irrigation

The capillary action differs in each wreath because moss and soil density vary, which initially calls for testing and adjusting in each case. As a safeguard, lay a thick, folded towel on a cookie sheet underneath the wreath to be watered, to catch drips and spatters. The following drip rates were effective in my wreath:

Drip Rates

Overnight . . . . . .one drop
every three seconds
One day . . . . . . .one drop
every five seconds
One week . . . . . .one drop
every ten seconds

Irrigation Tips:

🌿 If the moss has dried to a hard state and surface tension prevents absorption, apply a solution of one drop of water penetrant (an inert nontoxic liquid sold in nurseries) or liquid dish soap to one gallon of water to increase absorption efficiency.

RAIN

At times the gardeners in arid regions such as California and Arizona envy the soft rains of Seattle and Portland, but prolonged saturation is harmful to succulents. By hanging wreaths under the eaves or an overhang of a house, the amount of rainfall received can be controlled. Most of my customers in Florida utilize this method for rain as well as sun protection.

A temporary drape "umbrella" of a plastic drop cloth is another approach to the problem provided the plastic is propped so that it does not touch the wreath directly and is removed as soon as the rain ceases.

When I was a little girl, my grandmother and I would dash outside with the houseplants during the soft, warm, spring rains. I have been known to do the same with my wreaths. After the good wash and leaching of residual salts, the wreaths always perk up and look grateful. Wreath owners who live in areas where acid rains are common should check with their local weather stations and nursery experts for information on the pH quality of the rains in their immediate areas. Where rains are at an unhealthy-for-plants pH level, rinse your outdoor wreath with clear water immediately after an acid-rain shower.

TEMPERATURES

When frost warnings go out and temperatures go down, it is time to bring tender succulent wreaths indoors and place them in the brightest available daylight.

If the temperature drop is temporary and the wreath hanging on the outside wall of the house is too large and cumbersome to move, sufficient warmth can be trapped to prevent frost damage by draping a blanket in front of the wreath from the overhead eaves.

New cold-hardy wreaths acclimate to low temperatures after a six- to eight-week period when their root system is sufficiently established to withstand temperatures to 28 degrees Fahrenheit. The big danger to these wreaths is dehydration. Remember to irrigate sufficiently to prevent desiccation. Snow cover is ideal, unless the snow—as the rain in some areas—has a dangerously unbalanced pH level. Again, checking with regional experts is recommended.

In severe climates, protect sempervivums, sedums, and other cold-hardy succulents remaining in the garden by spreading a heavy mulch over them so that the heaving earth caused by the freeze and subsequent thaw won't expose their roots to drying. The same principle has been used by one customer in Wyoming who buried her wreath under a thick mulch and reported, "In spring it came back like gangbusters."

FERTILIZING

The wreath-base core of soil sustains succulents adequately on the wreaths for approximately two years. At that time, I start a dilute fertilizer schedule of one-quarter strength of a balanced fertilizer, such as Schultz-Instant Liquid Plant Food™ with its high potassium and phosphorous formula, that helps retain the plants' high-color and robust health. The one-quarter-strength solution sustains a healthy vigor without promoting a spurt of growth. I occasionally alternate with the same dilution of fish fertilizer, which is higher in nitrogen.

PRUNING

The succulents' sustained growth in the form of a wreath is slower than those grown in a garden or larger container, and pruning is minimal. When the plants begin to exceed the parameters of the wreath form, trim the growth to the first or second set of leaves, or sever the elongated rosette forms—leaving an inch stub to regenerate—and camouflage the exposed cut with other plant material.

New growth also produces plant material that can be replanted in the same wreath, garden, plant container, or another wreath. Many of my customers keep an additional prepared wreath base to receive the cuttings from their original wreath as a very personal gift-in-progress.

PEST CONTROL

Pests are few in a living succulent wreath. I only need manual controls: a brisk cold-water wash and a reasonable tolerance of insects "in residence."

Pest-Control Tips:

🌿 A dry, soft paintbrush is good for removing dust, aphids, and spider webs. Cotton-tipped swabs dipped in alcohol rid mealy bugs of their waxy protective coats. Follow the alcohol treatment with a clear-water rinse.

🌿 A few drops of liquid soap in cold water will help wash off aphids, mites, and other sucking insects.

🌿 Severe infestations of fungus gnats, although not harmful to plants, are very annoying. Gnats are attracted to moist moss for laying their eggs; the driest possible environment helps to discourage them. But the best and most environmentally safe control is a simple hand vacuum that sucks up the adult flies. Repeated regularly, the vacuum breaks up the cycle of hatching eggs over the next ten days, and the use of Diazonon™ and other toxic pesticides is avoided.

BIRDS

Birds are an occasional challenge but, for me, never a pest. Fluffy moss is tempting building material for nesting birds. Sparrows once set up a maternity ward on the crest of our large wreath, in safe repose from the family cat. Our daughter was expecting our first grandchild at that time, and the birds evoked immediate respect. We circumvented the area on tip-toe for the interim. Only when the fledgling youngsters took flight did I draw upon my reserve supply of moss to restore my wreath and remodel the former nursery.

ILLUSTRATION BY JESSE BAER

Chizu '88

From

Teddy Colbert's Garden
P.O. Box 9
Somis, CA 93066

9/20/95

© Teddy Colbert's Garden '95

EXPRESS

HANDLE WITH CARE

Frag

Chapter Eight
Receiving and Sending Wreaths

MAIL-ORDER LIVING WREATHS FROM TEDDY

We note "Live Plants, Open Immediately" on our shipping label. Even if you are unable to give further care to the wreath right away, open the box, remove the packing, and let the wreath breathe. Select a cool place out of direct sunlight for your wreath until you can follow the "Care of Your New Wreath" directions enclosed.

Wreaths are shipped fairly dry to prevent rotting in the enclosed carton. Water your wreath deeply if necessary (See Irrigation on page 116), and let it drain as directed, according to the method you select. Check for any cuttings that may have jostled loose; reinstall them in the method described under Installing the Succulents.

SENDING

Frequently my customers wish to give more meaning to a gift wreath by making it themselves, either from the clippings of their own mature wreath or from new materials. They often ask me how to ship them safely.

After six years of mail-order business experience, I assure them that, almost without exception, living wreaths do indeed ship well if a few precautions are taken.

FOLLOW THESE GUIDELINES:

1. Withhold watering for two to three days.

2. Obtain a rigid carton approximately two inches higher, wider, and deeper than the planted wreath.

3. For packing material, use balls made of crushed sheets of newspaper. Make a large quantity of these paper balls, and place one layer on the bottom of the shipping carton.

4. Wrap the newly planted wreaths in soft paper towels to hold the cuttings in place during the jostling of the trip. Lay

Crushed paper balls are effective "cushions," for shipping wreaths. This cold-hardy succulent wreath, like other wreaths, belies its delicate appearance and travels well.

three or four strips of attached paper towels out on the table like the spokes of a wheel. Place the wreath in the center; lift the towels up and over the outside and tuck them inside the wreath.

5. Place the towel-wrapped wreath, bottom side down, in the bottom of the carton. The legs of the spacers will create a space that prevents crushing of the bottom plants.
6. Fill all other empty spaces in the carton and on top of the wreath with the remaining paper balls, and firmly pack the corners. Don't be reluctant to pack it fairly tight; the wreaths are

tougher than they look. Enclose a brief note on new-wreath care to the receiver of your gift.
7. If it is an exceptionally large wreath, to prevent crushing from inevitable stacking, place a plastic nursery can in the wreath's center, a six-inch or one-gallon size depending upon the depth of the packing carton.
8. Seal the box with strong

shipping tape, and boldly label "TOP" near the shipping label. Draw arrows pointing up along the sides to avoid possible reverse handling.
9. Print "Open immediately" on your shipping label, and choose second-day delivery. Call ahead to see if your recipient will be home to receive the package on that day.

In "Our Lady of Lourdes" church, this 15-year-old community advent wreath was constructed on a 36-inch frame. The finished wreath is approximately four feet in diameter.

CHAPTER NINE
GREAT GROUP ACTIVITY

CREATING WREATHS AS A FAMILY OR COMMUNITY ACTIVITY

A bond occurs when a group creates a living wreath. The succulent cuttings planted in this topiary form become an investment in beauty that intrigues and beckons the return of all participants, who invariably exclaim, "Did I do that?"

Lack of skills or previous gardening experience is no deterrent. The many entry levels to creating a living wreath accommodate those whose abilities are limited. When extra help has been needed for more complex stages of base construction, I have been assisted by volunteers or staff. However active and enthusiastic the assembling of the living wreath is, the final product is always as beautiful as the spirit within the group of participants.

Please join us for

Wreath Making

Teddy helps school children begin a new tradition of a living advent wreath for Immaculate conception church in Los Angeles.

As a suggestion, and encouragement for sharing your living wreath excitement with others, I am listing some groups who have created living wreaths with me:

*Children and adults with
    developmental disabilities
Mentally ill homeless
    persons
Center for homeless women
Home for frail and elderly
Church communities
Schools
Disabled veterans
Association of Retarded
    Citizens
Garden clubs*

As fund raisers:
*Hospital Auxiliary
Girl Scouts
Botanical garden volunteers*

The wreaths made by a family or in a community group go beyond being lovely ornamentals. They have initiated traditions at holidays, weddings, and special occasions; healed and inspired as horticultural therapy; and provided a rewarding social experience for countless people of all ages. The living wreath encircles our spirit while embracing the beauty of nature.

An altar boy of St. Martins of Tours in Brentwood, California, lights candles on a wreath created for their church by Teddy and a class of developmentally disabled students.

PHOTO BY BILL BEEBE

PART TWO
FLORAL, EDIBLE, AND ORNAMENTAL LIVING WREATHS

PHOTO BY CHAD SLATTERY

CHAPTER TEN

ADAPTING THE BASICS TO OTHER PLANT MATERIALS

ALTERNATIVES TO SUCCULENT WREATHS

These alternative living wreaths provide a seasonal flair to your home and inimitable gusto to your cooking when you adapt the living succulent wreath basics to other plant materials. The quiet elegance of the all-white impatiens and lobelia wreath belies its impact, and the "kitchen door" accessibility of the mixed-herb wreath offers fresh flavors that beg for harvest: Italian parsley and chives for the morning's scrambled eggs or fresh thyme and sage for the evening's roast chicken.

This whole new spectrum of floral, edible, or other ornamental living wreaths has been made feasible by modifying the soil beforehand with water-retaining crystals and a complete controlled-release fertilizer. The same basic construction of the living succulent wreath is used with noted adaptions. For those making a special living wreath for the first time, it will be necessary to first study the basic method in Chapters 4 and 5, on pages 44 through and including page 59.

While the maintenance of most special wreaths is higher than that of the living succulent wreaths, it is still less than for traditional topiary.

SOIL MODIFICATIONS

If a living wreath is to sustain flowers, fruit, and lush green foliage, the demands for nutrients and water will exceed the meager diet of such succulents as the cliff-hanging *Dudleya hasseii* on Catalina.

Horticultural research, which has given us water-retaining crystals and controlled-release fertilizer to sustain growth for as long as nine months, has opened the door to this new gardening adventure.

Polymer Water-Retaining Crystals

These crystals are a non-toxic, nonhazardous product capable of holding approximately two hundred times their weight in water, and they are ideal for moisture-loving plants such as impatiens, violas, mixed lettuces, and ivy. The polymers cost approximately $.75 to $1.40 per ounce, but a small amount can do a big job. Follow the manufacturer's recommended amounts on the package, and add them to the quantity of soil suggested in the chart on page 36. These are mixed together with the fertilizer into the soil at least one hour before planting to allow full absorption of the water. As the crystals absorb the water and swell, they increase the bulk of the soil.

Controlled Fertilizer

A fertilizer formula consists of three symbols that represent the proportions of the major nutrients: N (nitrogen), which is used to develop healthy leaves; P

Topiary gardening is an entirely new experience when floral, ornamental, and edible plants replace succulents in the living wreath. Plan for nutritional and moisture requirements for ivy, herb, strawberry and other plants that are different than those needed by succulents.

(phosphorus), which aids the formation of fruit; and K (potassium), which is required for flower development. Because the flowering and fruiting formulas are higher in phosphorus and potassium, they have formulas such as 10-18-10 and 14-14-14. For evergreen wreaths such as mixed herbs, leaf lettuces, ivy, and spider

Place your impatiens or petunia wreath indoors or outside, as these vertical examples welcome guests with bright color.

plants, such high-nitrogen formulas as 17-6-10 are more appropriate.

As a rule, the water-soluble nutrients are in small, gelatin-coated capsules that release when temperatures are over 70 degrees Fahrenheit. At that temperature, plants are metabolizing at a faster rate. Different formulations have a release range of three, six, or nine months. Consult the directions on the package for the amount of fertilizer to add for each gallon of soil.

PHOTOS BY CHAD SLATTERY
LOCATION COURTESY OF UNDERWOOD FARM MARKET

Grown from seed and victorious survivor of a snail's snack, this rebounded specimen of 'Purple Wave' is ready to grace a wedding or summer-evening dinner party, or simply to enhance the garden view from a porch swing.

Plant Selections for Other Living Wreaths

Similar to selecting succulents, the wreath form and its position, whether vertical or horizontal, must be considered as well as the predictable mature form of the plant itself.

Compact plants with a rounded canopy, such as sweet alyssum and lobelia, are suitable for both vertical and horizontal wreaths. For a suspended horizontal wreath or candelabra, plants that have a natural drape, such as nasturtiums, dwarf sweet peas, cascading types of lobelia, and petunias, lend the most drama. One dramatic example is the new ground-cover-class petunia introduced as the 'Purple Wave,' an All-American Selection winner for 1995.

SELECTING THE PLANTS

Plant material that is very young, even before the flower color shows, is easier to plant and the most capable of making the adjustment to living in the wreath base. The ideal point for transplant to a prepared wreath base is just after the juvenile leaf stage when there are one or two sets of adult leaves.

How Many Plants Are Needed?

The plants are grown for effect as "container" plants with limited root space and soil similar to a hanging basket crammed with colorful geraniums. Wreath plants are spaced much closer than if they were growing in a garden. Intervals of every 3–5 inches, depending on the plant size, is not too close. Two factors determine the number of plants: the size of the wreath frame and the growth pattern of the plant. To maintain the open center of the wreath form and allow for the bouffant character of most flowers, I avoid using a frame smaller than one with a fourteen-inch outside diameter and prefer an eighteen-inch frame for creating a more majestically proportioned wreath.

As a guide, plan on 24 to 36 plants for a fourteen-inch frame and 54 to 72 for one that is eighteen inches across. Variations are noted in the list of plants. It is wiser to err on the side of over-planting, since it is easier to prune off excess plants, than it is to open up the wreath base to insert them later.

If it is necessary to eliminate plants from an already-planted wreath base, never pull them out because that might destroy part of the moss wrap. Cut them off just below the surface and allow the severed roots to become part of the fibrous matter of the soil.

"Crop" Insurance

"Crop failure" does happen, even in the most meticulously maintained wreaths. To allow for insect damage or the swift spectre of dampening off—an irreversible fungus attack—extra plants grown in terra-cotta pots provide not only some insurance of replacements, but they attractively extend the theme of the plants in your wreath to the surrounding area.

Planting Season

To determine the best time to make your living wreath, follow your seasonal experience in the garden, consult a good gardening book, or ask a knowledgeable local nurseryman.

Planning Outdoor Living Wreaths

The living wreaths can be planted with a single specimen, or can be mixed as if you were planning a "little garden." Select complementary colors, similar scale, and textures such as those of viola, lobelia, and sweet alyssum.

The proportions of each flower can be chosen to your preference or determined by the availability of plant material, which is often a pleasant surprise. After I discovered some lobelia starts in my own brick planter and sighted reseeded sweet alyssum in my neighbors' landscape, with permission I pricked out their seedlings and planted them with pansies in a wreath.

Planning Indoor Living Wreaths

Not only do living-wreath ideas appear in unlikely places, but one idea often leads to another. After I traveled back to Connecticut to tape a program segment on flower and ornamental wreaths with Martha Stewart for her television program, I realized how short their outdoor growing season is and began to explore wreath possibilities for gardeners who do not live in a climate as mild as mine. I discovered the resources of my own kitchen pantry: "Alfalfa sprouts! How quick, what fun and how healthy. How could I have ignored you?"

Then I thought, "Why stop at alfalfa seeds?" And from the organic treasures at our local seed store, I came home with a galaxy of other seeds to try.

Another possibility was looking right down at me from the top of the refrigerator: trailing pothos would feel right at home if I planted it at the bottom of the wreath base, encouraging it to climb freely up the wreath form.

I recalled a harrowing drive to Hana, on a visit to the island of Maui, Hawaii, when one of the welcome diversions was the sight of pothos growing wild in the jungle. There it grew profusely with leaves increasing in size as it stretched up to reach the rays of sun through the dense treetops. My immediate reaction was, "It's growing upside down!"

Draped over the side of the refrigerator, my domesticated pothos had fortunately not realized it had a reversed position in life.

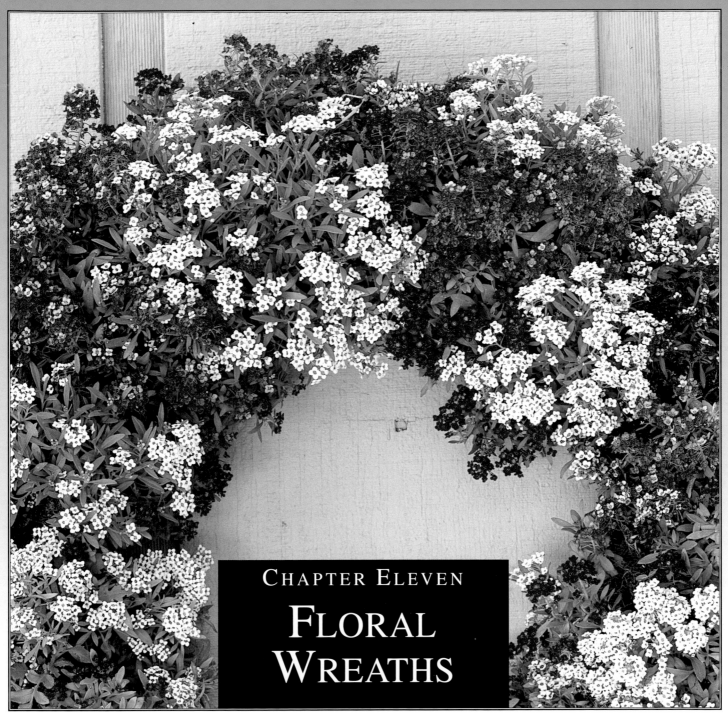

CHAPTER ELEVEN
FLORAL WREATHS

PHOTO BY CHAD SLATTERY

PLANTS AND TIPS FOR FLORAL WREATHS

I offer this list of plants out of my experience. Some I found by default and some found me. When I planted the "dwarf" nasturtiums for a wall wreath on the side of my breezeway, I envisioned an orderly circle of startling colors. The colors were startling—bombastic yellows, oranges, and glowing mahogany reds—but the tidiness went rampant. As the blossoms broke ranks, clambered toward my wisteria, and groped for the porch swing, I realized I had underestimated their determination to keep vining.

"All right," I complied, "I'll give you your freedom."

I turned the wreath over, hooked in some chains with a swivel hanger, and suspended it where my nasturtiums could cavort and dance in the wind.

The nemesia that I hoped would gently curve over the sides of a horizontal suspended wreath shot straight up to the heavens, and their base stems broke in the first gusty wind.

The following suggested plants are alphabetically listed in three groups and are coded:

"V" for vertical wreaths

"H" for horizontal table or centerpiece wreaths

"SH" to indicate suspended horizontal wreaths.

"Small" wreaths refer to those constructed on fourteen-inch frames, and **"large"** are those made with eighteen-inch frames. The grouping of the plants can also be flexible. Ivy can be used to fill in spaces between petunias or violas. The edible blossoms of violas and nasturtiums make these plants ideal to be added to culinary-herb wreaths for color.

In experimenting with living wreaths for more than a decade, Teddy has discovered the adaptability of a wide variety of plants for the vertical, horizontal, and suspended wreath forms discussed in this chapter.

PHOTO BY CHAD SLATTERY
LOCATION COURTESY OF OLD SOMIS BUNKHOUSE
OFFICES OF MARGUERITE WINGERT

Living Flower Wreaths

Impatiens wallerana—
Impatiens (V, H)
The burst of almost instant flowers of the dwarf strains of impatiens, 'Super Elfin' and 'Accent' almost make them seem bred for small and large wreaths. 'Peach Swirl' was the first impatiens wreath I made. It was an instant beauty that has not diminished in six months.

For the coming holidays, I look forward to introducing an all-white impatiens wreath, using it with traditional advent candles of three purple and one rose, then changing to red tapers for my Christmas Day buffet. I was glad I followed my nurseryman's caution of not using too much nitrogen in the fertilizer, which triggers excessive foliage and fewer flowers. My wreath has been sustained by one application of controlled-release 10-18-10 fertilizer. Expect to shape an impatiens wreath occasionally. By cutting just above a branch with flower buds, it will be it difficult to detect any pruning. If you are as frugal as I am, the clipping can easily be rooted

Background planting and filling in for mixing or recycling wreaths is easy with lobelia or alyssum.

in water and planted in another wreath, a flower pot, or your garden.

Lobelia erinus—
Lobelia (V, H, SH)
Lobelia was a joy to use, easy to plant, and the quickest to recover. It even looked better after transplanting. Root-bound nursery packs of lobelia, torn apart from the bottom of the root ball up, yield a plethora of plants after being divided. Their ability to root along the stem, called layering, is probably the secret to their rebound. I keep them very

90

moist during that early period after transplanting.

Generally, I use lobelia as a filler plant since I am partial to the vibrant blues. The lavender hues of lobelia seem difficult to integrate, but I am tempted to try a wreath composed solely of lobelia. Pure white lobelia is sublime combined with other all-white flowers and reminds me of old lace.

The cascading or trailing lobelia mature into foaming showers of color in suspended horizontal wreaths. It may be necessary to shop for a nursery with a broad lobelia selection to provide you with the color palette you prefer.

Seeds, of course, offer a superlative selection of color. Don't plan on using the seedlings for two months, however; they take an uncommonly long time to reach the transplanting stage.

Mimulus hybridus— Mimulus (V)

Mimulus was a new planting experience for me. In search of a flowering plant for the shade, I was introduced to 'Calypso Mix' mimulus by Diane Davis of Do Right Plant Growers in Saticoy, California. I liked the distinctive, exotic, orchidlike character in warm tones of gold, burnished orange, and wine red with amusing freckles and exquisitely blended bicolors. Mimulus is a water-loving plant that is a challenge in arid California but worth the effort to maintain it. Because of the bouffant form, I would recommend it only for large wreaths.

Tropaeolum majus— Nasturtium (SH)

To me, the nasturtium has no equal for the bombastic colors of orange, yellow, and deep red. The dwarf 'Tip Top' is a prime example. But if you prefer gentler tones, there is a new Thompson Morgan compact type called 'Peach Melba' that I am curious to try. On the eve of Saint Patrick's Day, the bouffant green leaves and first bloom seemed to anticipate my traditional celebration. The blossoms seemed to dance around the wreath: intense blue lobelia, sprightly deep purple, and clear yellow violas with wise little faces winking at me, and the nasturtiums in graceful swoops laughing.

"What," said those blazing orange rebels, "would your ancestors think of us?"

"I'll fix you; next year I'll just plant you with shamrocks."

Viola wittrockiana— Pansy (V)

Both pansies and violas, as members of the same plant family, prefer cool temperatures. A lot of sun is needed to keep the bloom cycle active, and if the flowers are sizeable, such as with the 'Jolly Joker,' the construction should be on a larger size frame.

If you start your own pansies from seed, bury them one-eighth of an inch deep in flats or pots; they need darkness to germinate. Transplant them to the wreath base when they have one to two sets of adult leaves.

The rebound of bloom in the viola family is amazingly responsive when all of the dead flowers are promptly and continuously removed. When pansies

I laughed out loud at the expressive orange "face" of 'Jolly Joker' and could hardly wait to show it to my grandchildren.

'Padparadja' pansy from the 100-year-old seed breeding firm of Ernst Benary was the All American Selection award for 1991. Below: 'Purplewave'.

occasionally succumb to dampening off, it is wise to replace them with other, less susceptible plants.

In spite of all the good garden sense I have gathered in twenty years as a garden writer, I still succumb to impulse buying. On a trip to a grower's nursery in Somis, months after the proper buying season for pansies, there was one overlooked flat in the rear of the display area. It was overgrown, root bound, slightly chlorotic, and already covered with dead flowers and seed pods. I should have passed it by,

but the color hit my eyes like a sling shot: deep, soft, rich, glowing orange. 'Padparadja,' chosen for the landscape at Disneyland's "Small World," had also left its mark on me. My fingers itched to take 'Padparadja' home. A treatment of dead-heading, top and bottom pruning, bloom-inducing fertilizer, then transplanting into a living wreath base—with white alyssum for texture and vivid blue lobelia for color balance—finally resulted in a show-worthy wreath, as well as a resolve to shop earlier.

Petunia hybrida multiflora—
Petunia (V, H, SH)
This species of petunia is preferred to *Petunia hybrida* Multiflora because the flowers, although smaller, are more numerous, and it is more tolerant of temperature extremes. A favorite Multiflora petunia is the lovely 'Chiffon Morn,' a blush pink and creamy white member of the Celebrity Series that was an All-America Selection (AAS) award winner for 1995. In contrast to other flowering plants that prefer a high proportion of potash and potassium, the other

AAS winner that year, 'Purple Wave,' responds well to a formula with a high proportion of nitrogen, according to researchers for the Pan American Seed Company.

Because 'Purple Wave' throws out remarkably long branches, it is ideal for suspended horizontal candelabras. When the growth is very young and pliable, the branches can be trained to grow on the outside of the wreath base by positioning them with shish kebab sticks.

Lobularia maritima—
Sweet Alyssum* (V, H, SH)
One of the marvels of living wreaths for nearsighted gardeners like myself is the proximity of the focus revealing exquisite but minute details that previously had only been enjoyed at our feet. How many of us realize that alyssum has fragrance? Delicate, almost ephemeral, but it is there.

Alyssum also responds to pruning and will give another surge of bloom if the flowering stems are removed before seed formation has taken

Luxurious 'Prelude' begonias were compatible with annuals as well as succulents.

over. Shade diminishes the bloom cycle of alyssum; full sun will increase flower production and deepen colors. The pure white alyssum is a great filler choice, but choose young seedlings or only the youngest transplants carefully. Mature specimens look tempting in the nursery but they invite failure.

For an Easter motif, try a door wreath planted entirely with the pink and purple tones in the 'Easter Bonnet' mix of alyssum. The display should easily extend to help celebrate Mother's Day. Living wreaths for these occasions make wonderful gifts. (See Receiving and Sending Wreaths on page 69.)

Lathyrus odoratus—
Sweet pea (SH)
I dreamed of billows of sweet peas clambering up and around a large wall wreath, planting them at the bottom third, then training them to grow in this manner. Easier said than done. There were several problems: first, I used the wrong type of bush sweet pea that grew straight up and wouldn't fill in the bottom of the wreath; second, the prevailing ocean wind brought dampness and

mildew; and third, by the time I learned my hard lessons, the planting season was over. Quit? Not at all.

For next season, I'll use the shorter-growing 'Bijou' sweet peas in a horizontal wreath. But images are addicting. Perhaps those of you readers who are successful in creating a living sweet pea wreath will write to me and share your secrets.

Viola spp.—
Violas (V, H, SH)
Violas bring a shower of delightful colors and charming little faces that seem to wink at you. Even now after their season passes, the images linger. Violas repeat their blooming more rapidly than their larger cousins, the pansies. Their diminutive scale is perfect for a living wreath. Because they have

'Blueberry Cream' and 'Lemon Chiffon' sorbet series violas are new and exciting plant specimens to feature alone in a living wreath or to combine with larger and smaller plants in a "mixed" plant wreath.

lucky components of both *Viola cornuta* and V*iola wittrockiana* species, they are more tolerant to extremes of heat and cold.

I was captivated both by the charm and the outstanding long performance in my violas wreaths of 'Lemon Chiffon' and 'Blueberry Cream' of the Sorbet series bred by Jaggei Sharma of the Waller Seed Co. I can hardly wait to start Sorbet again next season from seed, and I am eager to hear about the new violas on the plant breeders' horizon.

Chapter Twelve
Plants and Tips for Living Edible Wreaths

CULINARY HERBS

No matter how well stocked the kitchen spice cabinet cache of thumb-printed little tin containers, flour-dusted jars, and rust-flecked lids, you cannot have experienced the transcendence of seasoning food until you add freshly harvested herbs.

As an Easter/Passover season gift celebrating life and deliverance, I sent an herb wreath to a fellow gardener, friend, and great cook, Martha Stewart. Martha is no stranger to the wonders of the living wreath. In the letter sent with the gift, I described the new type of wreath that I called "The Cook's Rescue." The mixed herb wreath has literally

"delivered" us from many dull meals and evokes "Delicious!" from my husband, Ed. Bunching onions and the finer textured garlic chives flourish all around the parameter—wild, in its mockery, a perpetual "bad hair day"!

The herb wreath prompts extra attention to maintain the form, but I find that an advantage. After I groomed her wreath, we had dinner "on Martha" with the prunings going into a delightful marinara pasta sauce.

I had selected the

youngest seedlings and transplants I could find. For your own herb wreath, remember these "plant children" are simpler to plant and make an easier transition to their new home. If young herb plants are difficult to locate or if the choices are poor, I suggest starting a collection by seed. Similar to the flower wreaths, a larger quantity of plants is needed for a "Cooks Rescue" since their sustained growth results in smaller plants. Although you will not have the prolific growth as if they were in the garden, you can anticipate the same intensity of flavor and in quantities that I have always found adequate. If you can hang it in a

From 12 o'clock in clockwise order: Italian parsley, summer savory, cilantro, sweet marjoram, English thyme, 'Holts Mammoth' sage, dill, sweet basil, and chervil. Garlic and onion chives march around the perimeter in a wild 'bad-hair' day look. Opposite photo: mint wreath on the left, mixed herb on the right.

Clock

sunny spot just outside your kitchen door, celebrate your blessing for that proximity to your cooking area.

Suggested planting positions in parenthesis refer to **V**ertical, **H**orizontal, and **S**uspended **H**orizontal wreaths on page 88. When I prepare the soil for the base, I add the polymer, water-retaining crystals as well as a high nitrogen formula such as 17-6-10.

A good way to introduce yourself to the flavors of the herbs in your wreath is to make an herb topping of a single herb. Mince and crush a small amount of your favorite herb into room-temperature butter, oil, or sour cream and then sample it on that evening's baked potato.

THE KITCHEN RESCUE LIST
Anthriscus cerefolium —
Chervil (V, H, SH)
This spirited herb has a hint of tarragon and anise and is dear to the hearts of fine salad cooks. The chartreuse, lacy, and fernlike leaves are a visual delight in your wreath. Because chervil likes moisture, plant it in the bottom third of the wreath. Chervil likes cool weather and is all too short lived.

Healthy herb plants with young roots will transplant to a "kitchen rescue" wreath easily.

Coriandrum sativum —
Cilantro (V, H, SH)
If you are not sure if you have tasted cilantro, most likely you have not, though many restaurants garnish Mexican dishes with it. It is also known as Chinese parsley and coriander, and the flavor and aroma have a bang. Southwest cooks believe it is essential in a fresh salsa of tomatoes, chiles, and onions. When you shop for seeds, look for coriander, and the handiest place to find them might be on your own spice shelf or in the market. Cilantro is a warm-weather annual

herb with a quick life. To keep a crop growing in your wreath, poke seeds into the base periodically.

Chives
(circumference "bad hair")
Onion chives, (*Allium schoenprasum)* and garlic chives (*Allium tuberosum)* rebound considerably after "haircuts." Bunching onions are a good substitute for onion chives and have a final harvest of sweet little bulbs that are easy to snip off at the roots. While they are young, the slender grasslike blades of garlic chives have a remarkable flavor and an intense green color. I prefer them to garlic cloves, especially in stir-fry cooking, and have vowed to plant a much larger quantity next time.

This rambunctious planting—all around the circumference in little tufts pointing every which way—looked like my active little granddaughter's hair that, although it never stayed put, always looked endearing.

Anethum graveolens—
Dill (V, H)
I had my fingers crossed when I purchased the young herbs labeled "bouquet dill"

and hoped they would not bolt into the familiar tall, leggy plant but would remain dwarf. It did; helped, no doubt, by the confined growth in the wreath base. In welcome contrast to the other leaf forms in the wreath, the dill also had a feathery texture as well as the inimitable flavor of fresh dill.

When I think of dill, I think of its flavor in potato salad, in sour cream for baked potatoes, on fresh salmon, and for a fresh "wake up" flavor with tossed greens. The flavor of dill deteriorates rapidly when it is dried. After using the fresh herb, you probably will not want to use it any other way.

Petroselinum crispum —
var. *neapolitanum*
Parsley (V, H)
This flat-leafed Italian parsley has a rich flavor, and is far superior to *Petroselinum crispum,* or curly leafed parsley that, although the most popularly grown garden herb, is also the most neglected on the dinner plate. Whole fresh leaves of Italian parsley, chopped and sprinkled on salads, meats, or eggs, lend visual appeal as well as delicious flavor and high

amounts of vitamins A and C. This leggy plant calls for pruning in the wreath, but you will enjoy its frequent, last-minute addition to eggs, sauces, soups, chilies, stews, and stir-fries for fresh taste and bright color.

Satureja hortensis—
Summer Savory (V)
The annual, *Satureja hortensis*, is also called summer savory and has a gentler flavor than the more coarsely leafed perennial, winter savory. Its use is traditional with summer string beans. I always look forward to adding it to my favorite, flat, Italian pole beans. Summer savory grows tall and erect, but its ancestor is one of the components of 'Herbes de Provence' and is found in irresistible tapenade, an olive spread of that region. Its ability to be frequently harvested redeems its ungainliness.

The harvest may only be a snippet here and there but such magic! In an instant I have "Herbes de Provence" for my lunch! On a cool and very busy day, I heated a portions of canned chicken soup, turned off the flame, then stirred in equal parts of chopped fresh savory, rosemary, sweet marjoram, and oregano, put on the lid to capture the volatile oils, and called my husband, Ed, to join me for lunch. Ed sat down, sampled the soup, looked up and said incredulously, "Are you sure this isn't homemade?"

Origanum marjorana and *Origanum vulgare* —
Marjoram (V)
These herbs are so closely related that they even fool the experts. The Greek word from which the genus Oregano is derived means "joy of the mountain," which seems to punctuate its zest and affinity for tomato dishes such as pizza. Marjoram has a graceful, bountiful form in the wreath that seems to match the gentle flavor of its tender leaves.

Salvia officinalis—
Sage (V, H, SH)
Sage, the 'Holts Mammoth' in particular, is a favorite among herb gardener friends of mine. It is used in soups, chowders, poultry stuffing, and in our favorite sage-and-green-pepper cornbread. This distinctive herb has many other uses and was once considered very valuable. The Chinese eagerly traded four times a given amount of their tea for one similar portion of sage. I was surprised by the pleasant bracing flavor of brewed sage.

Ocimum basilicum—
Sweet Basil (V, H, SH)
Basil grown in my wreath seems to taste stronger and grow longer. The mobility of the wreath allows me to pamper this Mediterranean annual with a warm location and judicious nipping of flower heads to coax as long a production of leaves, especially if I leave two sets of leaves to help the plant regenerate.

In 1980 I conducted a survey for a *Los Angeles Times* feature among members of the Los Angeles Unit of the Herb Society of America about culinary herbs. On their list of favorites, sweet basil took first place. There is a wide array of other differently flavored basils, but even after many years of sampling and sniffing I still am slightly addicted to the "pungent aroma reminiscent of lemon, pepper, and clove. Fans love it in any tomato dish and herald it as the soul of pesto," I noted in *The Basic Herb Garden*.

Thymus vulgaris—
Thyme (V, H, SH)
English thyme is also unfairly called common thyme. "Common" is demeaning for such a plucky plant whose small, intensely flavored leaves produce such versatile food enhancement. If I could only have one herb to grow, it would be English thyme.

Sprinkle a pinch of crushed leaves on a boiled egg, and you will never miss the salt. Traditional use of thyme includes bouquet garni for soups and gravies, poultry stuffing, and seafood chowders. Thyme also gives an innovative lift to mashed potatoes and pea soup.

Mentha spp,—
Mint (12-11) (V,H)
Mentha species, and there are more than 600 of them, are naturals for vertical and tabletop living wreaths since their shallow root system is a circular series of runners. Mellow-flavored 'Mint The Best' is my own favorite. I was told this particular variety was the result of a world-

wide search by a tea company for the best brewing flavor.

There are two methods for constructing a mint wreath. Cut the stems and root them in water until they have a new root one inch long, and then plant them in the manner described on page 112 for rooted cuttings. The alternate method is to fill the mat of moss inside of the wreath frame halfway with soil. Uproot an established plant, or shake out a nursery pot; the roots will already be in a wreath formation. Cut back the mint stems to about two nodes above the runners to reduce transplant shock. Lay the runners on top of the soil in the frame, leaving the top two nodes outside the frame so that they extend beyond the frame when it is wrapped. (See column one on page 104 for instructions on wrapping transplants.)

LIVING SALAD WREATHS
Ideas for living wreaths come from unexpected sources. When I first arrived in Somis, an agricultural community, the nearby fields of leaf lettuce startled me with their striking bands of color: burgundy red; chartreuse; deep, rich, dark green; bronze; cool blue green. I could not believe they were all lettuces. The last time I saw such swaths of color was in Holland at tulip time.

I wondered how I might try them successfully in a wreath. Planting individual plants was one possibility and inserting seeds was another. Then it occurred to me to wrap the seeds inside the moss. I experimented with seeds sprinkled on the moist moss between frame wires, covered with soil mixed with high nitrogen controlled-release fertilizer and polymer crystals. The seedlings emerged right through the moss and soil as I had hoped. For detailed propagation instruction, see Seed on page 110.

Any leaf-lettuce seed is satisfactory, so your own personal favorites may be used. My own preference is toward the tender and sweet, nutty-flavored mâche variety, because it never seems to turn bitter—even as it begins to set seed. Ordinarily, mâche is a cool-weather lettuce. However, I learned from my seed supplier at Le Jardin du Gourmet in Vermont that the large-seeded type tolerates high temperatures. Our mâche wreath certainly retained its sweet tenderness through 90 degrees Fahrenheit and hotter summer days.

To capture the beauty of the lettuce field, I asked Le Jardin du Gourmet to prepare a special mix of seed to give me a spectrum of color and diversity of texture. Their assortment included the following:

Mâche A Grosse Graine
Mâche Verte de Cambrai
Mâche Ronde
  Mariachere
Lettuce 'Red Sails'
Lettuce Du Bon Jardinier
Lettuce Batavian Rouge
Lettuce Grosse Blonde
  Paresseuse
Lettuce Black Seeded
  Simpson
Lettuce Bronze Leaf
  Mignonette
Chicory Frise Rouge
  de Trevise
Chicory Frise Barbe
  de Capucin

Thin the seedlings for harvest by cutting off the lettuce plants at the base or transplant them to cover the outside edge of the wreath.

See page 110 for an explanation of geotropism. To prolong future crops, cut off the outside leaves of the rosettes. The cool weather in San Francisco extended the crop of one customer for almost three months.

Chenopiaceae —
Spinach (V)
Because the leaves of newer types of spinach are bred to grow smooth and straight to make washing the leaves easier, some of the flavor was sacrificed, and the arrowhead shape of the leaves did not complement the wreath base. None of the varieties in the seed racks had what I wanted; but then, in San Francisco I found an organic farmer selling her produce who had the rounded, deeply crinkled dark emerald green of 'Bloomsdale' savoy. I was given a leaf to taste, and my search ended.

Old-fashioned 'Bloomsdale' spinach has its challenges. Not only does it need cool weather to mature, but it will bolt to seed when the days of late spring lengthen and the weather warms. Sow it in the fall or winter in mild

climates and in spring for summer harvest where climates are severe. This spinach is best savored in quickly cooked recipes or raw in a salad. Either way it is a memorable taste experience.

As with the lettuces, soil prepared for spinaches requires polymer crystals and high nitrogen fertilizer.

Spinach Wreaths and Rose Bushes

Sixty years ago in an exquisitely tended rose garden, a little girl squatted next to a tall man. They planted spinach seeds around her grandfather's rose bushes— with his permission of course. Even though the little girl lived in his big house now, she was very sad. The Great Depression had caused her daddy's business to fail, and their little house had to be rented to support the family. The tall man, her Uncle Larry, tried to cheer her by asking what she missed the most. "My vegetable garden," she answered.

There was no room for a child's plot in the well-tended garden, but Uncle Larry was a landscape architect, and he used his ingenuity to design spinach wreaths around the rose bushes for his niece to plant and tend. Each day became more exciting; the first leaves were straight, almost like grass, but then came wonderful dark crinkly leaves that looked like crepe paper. She cut one at a time with her blunt-tipped scissors and carried them on a thick china plate into the kitchen. At the dinner table, her "Opa" tasted them, smacked his lips, and announced, "That was the best spinach I ever ate." The little girl looked forward to the next day in the garden, and the next.

The depression faded, the little girl grew up, and Teddy the business woman still makes spinach wreaths and looks forward to the next day in her garden.

Making a Sprout Wreath

While it is very short lived, a sprout wreath is embarrassingly easy to create and could well be a normal step in making any size wreath base for all kinds of living wreaths. See Recycling the Living Wreath on page 117.

The first step in either of two methods is to make sure the finished wreath base has a very close "haircut" or the furry strands of the sphagnum moss wrap will end up being harvested along with your food. For smaller seeds such as alfalfa, clover, and Chinese cabbage, roll a thoroughly soaked base, top down and on its sides, in a tray evenly sprinkled with your choice of seeds. The extra-wet seeds can be slathered onto the inside surfaces of the wreath base by depositing them in a wiping manner with your fingers. Once the moist wreath base has accumulated a thorough coating of seeds, slip the base into a clear plastic bag and leave in a bright but not direct light. Keep the base moist by gently spraying until the seeds sprout. When the roots anchor the sprouts, remove the bag. Regularly spray and rotate the wreath toward the light to promote lush, uniform growth.

For larger seeds such as sunflowers, peas, aduki beans, mung beans, lentils, and wheat, sprinkle the seeds on the moist moss between the wires of the frame. Smaller seeds can be mixed with the large seeds and will sprout through the moss with them. Roll the finished base in some seeds to cover the sides and defy the law of geotropism.

Place the sprouted wreath on the lunch table, and complete the inviting arrangement with garden scissors at each place setting for anyone who likes to harvest their own "crop" and add them to a sandwich, stuffed avocado, chicken or seafood salad.

The sprout seeds take from three to five days to sprout, and continue for almost two weeks, if they are not eaten. If they grow too fast, harvest your sprout crop with scissors and refrigerate in a sealed plastic bag. Our sunflower sprouts got ahead of us and reached eight inches in height, but they still were delicious.

Alfalfa sprout wreath, seed to the table in six days! Amazing.

MAKING A FRUIT WREATH
Fragaria x Ananassa—
Strawberry (1-5, 7-11)
(V, H)

The winter bareroot season is the time to shop for dormant strawberry plants. A dozen plants for a medium wreath and two dozen for the large is a good number to work with, but include some extra for container growing, and hope they will lure the birds away from the wreaths. Select an everbearing, day-neutral variety that suits your climate.

Soak the roots in water while you prepare the wreath base and mix the polymer crystals and a high P K fertilizer into the soil to boost the fruiting. After you place the frame on the moist moss, put the heads or crowns of the strawberries far enough outside of the frame that they will be above the moss after wrapping. This procedure will prevent rotting. Lay out their bare roots within the wires and cover them with soil. Repeat a second layer in the same manner, staggering the crowns between those of the bottom layer. Keep the top focus in mind as you plant. Avoid placing the heads in the 6 o'clock posi-tion where the runoff of irrigation water could rot them. Wrap the moss in the manner described under Transplants on page 114.

The 'Sequoia' strawberries I planted in January were attractive from the first dark green shoots that appeared within the month. Blossoms followed quickly, and by April, luscious red fruit had developed. The berries needed protection from the sharp-eyed birds. On Father's Day in June, the increased fruit production of the 'Sequoia' was so tempting that my littlest grand-daughter didn't even bother to pick off the fruit but bit into it, right on the stems in the wreath.

(Fragaria vesca,
Fraises des bois)—
Wild Strawberries
It took a king to bring these "strawberries of the forest" out of the woods. In 1346, King Charles V of France ordered the transplanting of 1,200 wild strawberries into the royal gardens at the Louvre in Paris. They were and still are prized for their white flowers, aromatic small, red, wine-flavored fruit, and shiny green foliage, all of which are shown off to perfection in a living wreath.

Bareroot plants are offered by some seed catalogs but they are not cheap, and a large number are needed for good coverage in a wreath—two to three dozen in the medium size

Tomatoes brighten salads with color and flavor.

and at least four dozen in the large. It is very easy and most economical to grow your own seedlings. Seeds germinate best when they are exposed to bright but not direct sunlight at 70 degrees Fahrenheit. See the Seed and Seedlings section on page 110 for the best propagation technique and Sources at the end of the book for seed catalogs.

A few berries can add an elegant touch on the top of a fruit cup garnished with a sprig of mint, a dish of frozen yogurt, or a creamy custard. A fresh strawberry or two makes a glass of chilled white wine a classy accompaniment to any festive occasion.

Tomatoes (2,5,7,10)
The tomatoes selected for a wreath should be a dwarf variety. Although I have tried 'Micro Tom,' I did not think the flavor worth the effort. After some research, a competing seed company admitted the only dwarf tomato with good flavor was 'Tumbler,' bred specifically for hanging baskets by Simon Crawford for The Pan American Seed Company. The seeds germinated in four days and were transplanted into the wreath base three weeks later. The Thompson Morgan seed catalog suggested 55 days to fruit. The red tomatoes had a delicious, slightly sweet, true tomato flavor and produced fruit for the longest period of any tomato in my garden.

Chapter Thirteen
Living Ornamental Wreaths

PHOTO BY TEDDY COLBERT
PLANTS COURTESY OF MANNY SINGER, 11 DWARF SPECIES OF *SANSEVIERIA*

LIVING ORNAMENTAL WREATHS

Unless otherwise noted, the soil for all the ornamental wreaths was prepared with polymer, water-retaining crystals and a high nitrogen controlled-release fertilizer.

Hedera helix —
English Ivy (V, H, SH,)
Depending upon whether it is hardy or tender stock, English ivy can be grown indoors or outdoors. The smaller leaf varieties look better on the medium wreaths, but because there are so many ivies to choose from, there is an ivy for every size and style of wreath. Topiary societies offer a wealth of information (See Sources on page 124).

I feel a little sheepish expressing my newfound enthusiasm for this plant. When The National Ivy Society cosponsored their national conference with the San Diego Zoo in 1991 and invited me to exhibit with thirteen other topiary artists,

I accepted—with an apology: "But I don't even like ivy!" They promptly and graciously absolved me, explaining that they knew about my preference for succulents, but it was my technique that they were acknowledging as a new topiary art form.

At the show, the weather suddenly turned quite hot and the "newcomers"—the upstart living succulent wreaths—came through unscathed while life-size ivy topiaries of elephants, gorillas, and other forms had a first-day-at-the-beach type of crispy sunburn.

My source of the plant material for the ivy wreath was our dining-room plant brought from our other home. The branches had exceeded their pedestal height and trailed on the floor. A trimming was in order to prevent anyone from tripping. Twenty-four of those healthy tip cuttings went into individual jelly jars filled with water on the window sill above the kitchen sink. Four days later, they each had a new one-inch root and were planted into a prepared wreath base. Soon, new shoots made their appearance. As the shoots grew longer, I pinned down the new length with a topiary fern pin, and they obediently put a new root down at that contact. That was fun. I was a traditional "topiarist," and—with ivy!

Epipremnum aureum —
Pothos (2-10) (V, SH)
Although the lesson learned in the forest outside Hana on Maui Island taught me that pothos is a vine and is meant to climb up, I had always hesitated because the only climbing device I was familiar with was ugly. The fiber composite pole

commonly used in the middle of the container, reminded me more of a cat-scratching pillar than a tropical jungle. I wondered how pothos would like to climb up a vertical wreath. Reluctant to dismantle my own "upside" trailing pothos growing in reverse to its natural habitat direction, I bought a five-inch pot of pothos thick with leaves for four dollars at a local nursery, expecting to root lengths of the branches in water. To my surprise, when I tipped out the new plant, I didn't have a mature thick plant at all. The eighteen newly rooted cuttings jammed in the pot seemed planned more for me than someone who wanted to grow a healthy houseplant. The plants were rescued from a sickly maturity. I felt like a hero.

The roots were eased into large slits made mostly toward the lower portion of the wreath base. To help train the pothos leaves into a circular direction, I secured the stems with shish kebab sticks and fern pins, anchoring them at the nodes where they promptly put out new roots. The first pothos wall wreath I made was on a frame of fourteen inches, but

I would like to attempt a larger one and also a suspended horizontal wreath; but then, that would be ignoring what I learned from the forest in Hana.

Oxalis acetosella—
Shamrocks (V, H)
This oxalis is one of many plant forms sold as "shamrocks" around Saint Patrick's Day. I planted it partly as a retort to the orange nasturtiums that dared to bloom for me on that green-focused holiday.

My revenge backfired and led to a discovery of a stalwart shade of houseplant that survived radical root pruning during transplanting, weathered a fungus attack of rust, and has never stopped blooming. In the fall, I'll replant the little dormant bulbs for another attempt at creating a real Irish beauty.

Chlorophytum comosum 'Variegatum'—Spider Plant (V, SH)
In three corners of what we call the garden room, off the dining area and above the window seats, I suspend bouffant spider plants. The television is in the fourth corner. Our sons are tall, and when they visit, they lounge, watch football games, and attack the bowl of guacamole and chips in front of them.

They complained that the "spiders" interfered with the touchdowns. Three dozen spider plantlets were promptly trimmed off, allowing the mother plants to perk up without the demands of all those babies.

Out came the box of jelly jars used for the ivy cuttings, and a parade of "spiders" took their place on the window sill above the kitchen sink. In six days they all had new roots growing out of the old air roots and were ready to be planted into a large wreath base. Wide slits made with the flat end of the forceps, parallel to the copper wire wrap and crossbars, allowed me to slip in the new root and the air roots together deep into the cavity without damaging them.

The newly installed spiders lovingly embraced the curved wreath base, and their striated green-and-white leaf pattern accented their wreath position beautifully. The wreath was kept in a horizontal position for a week to allow the newly installed plants to settle. I'm awaiting their maturity, when they will begin to throw out new flower stems to form other

Bouffant spider plants add texture and beauty to an interior room where light is sufficient.

Pothos climbing as nature intended, up and around the living wreath base.

plantlets. Depending upon what the wreath looks like with trailing plantlets, I'll decide how much to prune or even convert to a horizontal suspended wreath. There is always the compost, or another wreath.

The wreath mystery: countless family members and guests have viewed my spider plants hanging in the corners. "Nice room," first timers say. But when the wreath was hung on the wall, the generic response was, "Wow!" Their glance was drawn and held. Yet the plants were the same, the room was the same. The added magic was the living spider wreath.

Plectranthus nummularis— Swedish Ivy (SH)
I do not have the place for Swedish ivy now, but at one time I was very enamored of this resourceful plant. For my son's quarters as a resident assistant at Irvine University, I constructed a "waterfall" arrangement by hooking three cascading Swedish ivy plants to one another and hanging it from a corner ceiling hook. I felt the massed plant made the best of the limited space in his college room and gave him a cheery touch of home— strictly a parent's interpretation.

I have not made a wreath of this plant yet, but I can picture the crisp, shiny leaves pouring out of suspended wreaths in the same loose "waterfall" and lit with candles for a dinner party or for the holidays. A wreath base with four candleholders would be an innovative advent wreath, and the larger size with nine candleholders could serve as a menorah.

Swedish ivy tip cuttings are easy to propagate in water or vermiculite (See Rooted Cuttings on page 112). I can recall preparing an untold number of plants in Dr. Crummett's greenhouse at UCLA to sell and raise funds for the horticulture department.

CHAPTER FOURTEEN

PLANTING TECHNIQUES FOR ALTERNATIVE WREATHS

PLANTING ALTERNATIVE LIVING WREATHS

There are several types of plant materials used in propagating a living wreath; they range from seed to pot-bound plant cuttings. A ratio describes the effort: ease is directly proportionate to vision, which means that the youngest plant form (the seed) is the easiest to plant yet calls for the most vision. Pot-bound plants with their bloom require less vision but are the most difficult to install in a prepared wreath base.

Whatever method is used—seed, seedling, rooted cutting, or transplant—I allow the wreath base to rest in a horizontal position for about a week after being planted. Keep the base in a bright light to facilitate germination, rooting, and sprouting, but protect it from strong sunlight during that period to prevent harming the delicate starts.

SEED
Vision is a catalyst to the final image and wreath making is never boring. In every stage from winter catalog dreams to final impact, one stage leads to another: the seed emerging, the juvenile leaves, the adult leaves, transplanting, budding, and then the grand finale of flowers or herbs. Vision becomes a virtue and the cost is in pennies.

There are two ways to plant seed in the living-wreath base. One method is direct planting in holes poked strategically in the base. The second and quicker method is to have the seeds emerge through the moss wrap, a better method for small seeds. With either approach, planting extra seeds is an insurance, and the superfluous plants are easy to snip off later. Birds and bugs can demolish seedlings quickly, and another transplant from a container or garden can rescue a wreath project.

Expect to contend with the law of geotropism—a big word for a simple concept that I had forgotten about, even though root-view boxes are used actively as part of Gardens For Kids Inc., a foundation that I cofounded in 1992 to support gardening education. We show children the effect of positive geotropism when plants respond to gravity: by sending roots toward the earth's center, their stems and leaves grow away from the main plant in what is called negative geotropism.

The children grasp it immediately, but I needed a reminder. I kept trying to get my seeds in the wreath to grow sideways against the forces of nature. Seeds put outside the wreath frame before wrapping still grew straight through the base to the top surface. To circumvent this tendency, I planted large curved-leaf lettuce and spinach varieties that would flop over the sides, or later poked seedlings into the empty side area. The alfalfa sprout wreath was easy because I could roll the sides of the wreath base in a tray of seed, but with the mixed sprouts I tolerated their erratic growth as I would a teenager's Mohawk hair cut.

DIRECT SEEDING
To implant larger seed types such as sweet peas and nasturtiums in a completed wreath base, make slits in the moss parallel to the copper-wire wrap using the end of a forceps or a kitchen knife. With the pincers, insert seeds 3/4 inch deep every four inches so that they have contact with the core of soil. When planting a vertical wreath, I concentrate the seeds at the lower one-third of the base and place them just under the center face to avoid where they would rot in the constant moisture that gravity encourages underneath.

If the stems are the vining type, train them to cover the upper portion while they are young and pliable, directing them around the top and continuing down the other side.

For a medium horizontal wreath, I space the seeds evenly over the top and outer

This sweet basil seedling is ideal for transplanting with its first true leaves and healthy roots.

110

1 1 1

side surface, and for a large wreath I extend the spacing of seeds to the top portion of the inside circle.

EMERGING SEED

Sow small seeds like spinach, lettuce, or sprouts directly onto the mat of moist moss. Place the frame in the middle of the mat and sprinkle the seed evenly within the frame wires and one inch on the outside and inside. Invert the frame with soil and wrap with moss as explained in the basic instructions on page 110. Lay the wreath base flat and keep moist. The germinating seeds will emerge through the moss wrap.

SEEDLINGS

Fill a four-inch nursery pot to the brim with sterile propagation mix or coarse vermiculite. This fascinating inert material of mica particles has been subjected to 2,000 degrees Fahrenheit and exploded by steam to hold four times its weight in water. Level it off with a piece of wood or ruler; then water it gently until the water runs out the bottom. Water it again with a half-strength fertilizer so that mature seedlings will have some nutrition waiting

there for them. Space the seeds evenly in the prepared propagation mix. Tent a clear plastic bag over the pot, propping it so that it does not touch the surface and will act like a little greenhouse to speed germination. Water the seeds only from the bottom by setting the pot in a dish or disposable baking pan so as not to disturb them. The water will be drawn up swiftly by the vermiculite. When the pot has absorbed as much water as possible, dump the remaining water out to avoid the rotting of delicate feeder roots when a plant sits in water.

After the appearance of leaves, remove the plastic bag—by degrees—to acclimate the seedlings to the drier air. The best time to transplant seedlings is after the second set of adult or true leaves has formed. Open a wide hole in the wreath base and, holding the seedling by the leaf, drop the roots into the cavity. Close the hole by pushing the moss toward the stem with your finger and inserting the tip of the forceps parallel to the stem as resistance. Gently push the moss and the stem together. Water after trans-

planting to the wreath base, and allow the wreath to rest in a horizontal position for about a week. To allow the roots to secure themselves in their new home.

ROOTED CUTTINGS

As a rule, I prefer rooting cuttings of ivy, Swedish ivy, pothos, spider plants, and impatiens in water until the new root is about one inch long. A brittle, longer root is difficult to handle and has more difficulty adapting to soil. When pruning the impatiens wreaths, I occasionally root the cuttings as a fill-in supply or use them to plant another wreath.

Vermiculite can be used as the rooting medium or a commercial propagation mix of milled peat moss, perlite, and starter nutrients. For woody plants such as rosemary, propagate tip cuttings by trimming off the bottom leaves of the cuttings so that two nodes are exposed, then dip them in a rooting hormone, which is available at nurseries. Make sure the rooting hormone covers the nodes, while avoiding contact with your skin.

I use recycled six-plant pony packs to root the cut-

tings and slip each pack into a clear plastic bag, tented as described in the directions on seedlings. In three weeks, depending upon the degree of warmth. Look for roots showing at the bottom drain holes to make sure they are established. Transplant them into a wreath base described in the next paragraph.

Make a slit into the moist wreath base parallel to the wire wrap and ease in the cutting carefully so as not to damage the vital growth tip of the root. A long pair of tweezers or forceps is ideal for the delicate handling. As a wise precaution for avoiding skin irritations, remember to slip on surgical gloves when you handle the sphagnum moss (See Sphagnum Moss on page 36). A snug fit is helpful in leak-proof gloves to maintain the "feel" of handling the delicate plants and their hair-fine roots.

YOUNG TRANSPLANTS

When purchasing transplants, I think of how resilient young children are to new surroundings. Young plants are the same. Select healthy plants that have loose roots and are still in bud, with little flower color, to be the most

adaptable and easiest to handle. If the root ball is small enough, gently squeeze it to fit the slit in the base and ease in the roots with a forceps in the same manner as the rooted cuttings described above. The roots of impatiens are especially fibrous and easy to transplant in this manner. Martha Stewart and I demonstrated this for her television series.

No matter how carefully you handle the root ball, however, you are bound to damage the hair-thin feeder roots. There is a very sound principle that I learned in horticulture class: top pruning should equal bottom pruning. Because transplanting inevitably damages the root, and proportionate top pruning reduces the work load they have to sustain, plant setback is theoretically avoided. Take great care with the delicate roots of young transplants and they will recover their growth quickly.

OLDER, ROOT-BOUND TRANSPLANTS

Older plants that have been in the container too long are virtually impossible to fit into an opening in the finished base. But, here is a treasured, newly learned technique that helps salvage them. Wash the dirt off the root ball to reduce its size without damaging the roots; then, with forceps, ease the roots into the widened slit you have made in the wreath base. Another method is to install the entire plant around the inside and the outside of the frame. Because of this added bulk, and in order to maintain an open wreath form, consider using one of the bigger frames, especially if the flowers are also large. In contrast to the basic wreath construction, reverse the position of the frame on the mat of moss with the top side up rather than upside down. If preparing a custom frame, place the legs down, and the candleholders on top. Fill the frame with soil.

Sprightly blooms, with a bit of luck, grace shamrocks' symbolic trifoliolate leaf.

Loosen the root ball at the bottom with a fork and top prune the plant in proportion to the root mass that has been damaged in the transplanting process. Pinch off any flowers and seed pods to lessen the demand on the plant. Arrange the plants around the inside and outside of the frame, marching fashion, shoulder-to-shoulder in a double row, filling soil in the open spaces and exposed root area to prevent the plants from drying out.

Lift the moss from the mat, up and over the root balls, as described on page 46 for the basic wreath construction. Tuck moss around the crown of each plant from your patch pile if more coverage seems necessary. Review coiling the copper wire around the base in the basic construction directions, taking care not to cut into the tender stems and crossing the wire in an "X" at the back of the base to get as close to the necks of the plants as possible. This is the most difficult method and is my last resort when no other source is available, and I am compelled to pay the price for falling in love with yet another plant.

CHAPTER FIFTEEN
CARE AND MAINTENANCE FOR ALL LIVING WREATHS

MAINTAINING THE LIVING WREATH

The maintenance for other special living wreaths is basically the same as for that of the living succulent wreath, except there are more procedures to be followed. More moisture and fertilizer are the two significant demands that differ from dealing with succulents, and the consequent rapid growth of these plants calls for more frequent pruning.

IRRIGATION

Follow the dunk, dribble, or drip methods in the Care and Maintenance section, but be aware that the wreaths are considerably heavier than the succulent wreaths because of the polymer water-retaining crystals. Since their weight makes them difficult to lift off and submerge in water, I rely considerably on drip-irrigation bag sets described on page 67. For the wreaths I can lift comfortably, I have a "top dip" technique when I am in a hurry. I submerge the top half of the vertical wreath in a plastic-lined box, then hang it up, and let gravity water the lower portion.

FERTILIZING

The slow-release fertilizer helps to fortify their confined state, and as they mature I augment their nutrition with periodic one-quarter strength fertilizer in their irrigation water. Fish emulsion is a frequent choice for excellent nourishment. Fertilizer applications may be simplified by using drip-irrigation bags (See on page 115), an adaptation of a technique used by commercial nurseries that continually feeds plants in minute proportions measured in parts per million (ppm).

Preparing a place for your living wreath to drip after irrigation may change as your wreath grows and requires an expanded space.

PRUNING

The simple task of dead heading to keep seed pods from forming results in a dramatic profusion of bloom on living-wreath plants. With annuals such as pansies, violas, and petunias, nature's surge of energy to reproduce keeps flower production in high gear. When the seeds are formed, a signal goes out, "I've done my job, I quit," and flower production halts.

To keep the identifying open center of the wreath in its uniform parameter, occasional pruning is necessary. Petunias and impatiens especially benefit from pruning. With the mixed-herb wreaths, pruning provides the double benefit of prolific growth and dinner plans according to the prunings.

PEST CONTROL

The elevation of a wreath foils most crawling insects, but birds can spy wild and cultivated strawberries from astounding heights. I use a protective net to guard the crop before an event, but other than that, it's "Help yourself," guests—including birds—included.

PHOTOS BY CHAD SLATTERY

THE RECYCLED WREATH BASE

"What do I do when the flowers are gone and I've eaten the lettuce?" Your wreath base is a valuable resource and can be replanted with seeds or young seedlings for a new look and purpose. A customer at the San Francisco Landscape Garden Show, who was passionately fond of nasturtiums, vowed on the spot of her purchase to maintain those favorite flowers by continually poking more seeds into the base of the wreath. Perhaps with the cooler climate of her area she may be lucky enough to fulfil her intention.

Mixed-herb wreath near the kitchen door, guarded by Buster. Previous page:
As these annuals complete their season, it is a comfort to know that the beauty of my wreath can continue with other seasonal flowers, perennial ivy, or show remarkable compatibility combined with succulents.

I prefer to combine other plant material into recycled wreaths. My favorite choice is the stalwart succulents that offer not only longevity and ease of propagation from cuttings but a bounteous range of form and color for amazingly complementary replacements. In severe climates, when the outdoor growing season bows out to fall, the living wreath of annuals or herbs can be converted to an indoor wreath with rooted cuttings of ivy or lower-light succulents that adapt to bright indoor light conditions.

Your recycled living wreath can always be alive and lovely.

Discovery of this compatible complexity of succulents growing amiably with annuals and perennials was like successfully hosting a party of great friends who had never met each other before, yet seemed to bring out the best in each other.

PHOTO BY TEDDY COLBERT JR.
LOCATION COURTESY OF DR. AND MRS. ROBERT ANDERSON

PART THREE
COMING FULL CIRCLE

119

CHAPTER SEVENTEEN
THE SPIRIT OF CONTINUITY

Epilogue: Permanence and Pride

Thomas Hardy said in *Far from the Madding Crowd*, "Here at least the spirit of the ancient builders was at one with the spirit of the modern beholder . . . the eye regarded its present usage, the mind dwelt on its past history, with a satisfied sense of functional continuity throughout—a feeling of gratitude, and quite of pride, at the permanence of the idea which had heaped it up." So it may be said of my living wreaths.

Seven years ago, when my oldest son became engaged, he constructed a wreath for his fiancee's family as a Christmas gift. Displayed on the door of the 100-year-old barn, the living wreath reflects the innovative spirit of pioneer farmers and their wives who ventured, with brave hearts and open minds, from other continents to plant their orchards, build their barns, raise their families, and form new communities. In the late afternoon sun, the living wreath reconciles pioneer innovation with the new art form, complementing the venerable beauty of the old barn. The wreath and the barn are both well constructed and maintained.

The scale of this magnificent wreath, with its rugged texture, is obvious next to Teddy. The wreath is in harmony with the rugged door, celebrating the pioneering spirit that created both the barn and the art form.

122

SOURCES FOR LIVING WREATH MATERIALS

PLANTS AND SEEDS

Plant and seed material used to create living wreaths can be found in the following catalogs. Some of the more difficult items to locate are noted for your convenience. Catalogs are free unless otherwise stated.

LIVING WREATH INSTRUCTION AND SUPPLIES

Teddy Colbert's Garden
P.O. Box 9
Somis CA 93066
1 (800) TEDDY 81
E-mail:
  teddyc@ix.netcom.com
Web site:
  www.livingwreath.com
From the originator, planted living wreaths to purchase or make; easy ready-to-plant wreath bases, exclusive frame kits with hidden candle-holders, succulent cuttings. Author-inscribed award-winning book, The Living Wreath. Visit web site www.living-wreath.com or send SASE for free price list.

PLANTS

Abbey Gardens & Cactus
P.O. Box 2249
La Habra CA 90632
(310) 905-3520
Mail order only, exceptional collection of rare and unusual, mostly tender succulents. Will recommend plants for wreaths on request. Catalog $2, deductible from first order.

Squaw Mountain Nursery
36212 SE Squaw Mountain
  Road
Estacada OR 97023
(503) 630-5458
(503) 630-5849 fax
Exceptionally large, cold-hardy sedum and sempervivum plant collection. Catalog $2, applies to first order.

SEEDS

J. L. Hudson Seedsman
P.O. Box 1058
Redwood City CA 94064
Wild strawberry seeds.

Le Jardin du Gourmet
P.O. Box 75
St. Johnsbury VT
  05863-0075
Their 25-cent sampler herb- and lettuce-seed packets suit the amounts needed in living wreaths. They have an exciting collection of French seed, including mâche, with hot- and cool-weather varieties and 'Bloomsdale' Savoy spinach. The catalog is free, but for $1, it will be sent with 5 packets of herb seed. Bare-root wild strawberries are well-priced.

Thompson and Morgan
P.O. Box 130
Jackson NJ 08527-0308
'Tumbler' tomato, 'Purple Wave' petunia, wild strawberry, flower, herb seeds, 'Peach Melba' nasturtium.

PLANT SOCIETIES AND BOTANICAL GARDENS

Cactus and Succulent Society of America, Inc.
P.O. Box 35034
Des Moines IA 35034
Membership $30 per annum USA. $6 for spouse, foreign countries. $35 for bimonthly journal with "Cacti and Succulents for the Amateur" feature.

For additional information and schedule of nearest local chapter, contact the following:

Seymour Linden, Ph.D.
1535 Reeves Street
Los Angeles CA 90035
(310) 556-1923

American Horticultural
  Society
7931 E. Boulevard Drive
Alexandria VA
  22308-1300
(703) 768-5700
A nonprofit organization dedicated to excellence in horticulture. Dues $45 per year include subscription to 12 issues of American Horticulturist.

Botanical Garden
The Huntington Botanical
  Gardens
Desert Collection
1151 Oxford Road
San Moreno CA 91108
(818) 405-2141
One of the world's largest collections of succulents and cacti in the landscape and conservatory.

BIBLIOGRAPHY

Evans, Joan. *Nature in Design.* London: Oxford University Press, 1933 (p. 84).

Folklard, Richard, Jr. *Plant Lore, Legends and Lyrics.* London: S. Low, Marston, Searle and Rivington Publishers, 1884 (p. 36).

Freedburg, David. *The Origin and Rise of Flemish Madonnas in Flower Garlands,* 3rd ser., vol. 32. Münchner: Jahrbucher der Bildendenkunst, 1981 (p. 122).

Hardy, Thomas. *Far from the Madding Crowd.* New York: New American Library, Penguin Books,, 1982 (p. 38).

Mellencamp, E. H. "Renaissance Classical Costume: 1450–1515." Ph.D. diss. in 2 vols., University of Michigan, n.d. 1956 (p. 62).

Pliny the Elder. *Natural History,* 4th rep., vol. 21, rep. Second Chapter. Trans. by W. H. S Jones. London: Harvard University Press, Cambridge, Massachusetts, 1989.

Pulleyn, Robert. *The Wreath Book.* New York: Sterling Publishing Co., 1988 (p. 10).

Rothery, Guy C. *Decorator's Symbols, Emblems and Devices.* London: The Trade Papers Publishing Co. Ltd.; New York: The Painters Magazine, 1907 (p. 34).

Santino, Jack. *All Around the Year, Holidays and Celebrations in American Life.* Urbana and Chicago: University of Illinois Press, 1994 (p. 210).

Von Boehn, Max. *Modes and Manners: From the Decline of the Ancient World to the Renaissance,* vol. 1. London: G. G. Harrap Publisher, 1932 (p. 207).

ADDITIONAL SOURCES
These books are like dependable old friends; I recommend them for basic and regional gardening information:

Johnson, Hugh. *Principles of Gardening.* New York: Simon and Schuster, 1984.

Reader's Digest Illustrated Guide to Gardening. Pleasantville, New York, and Montreal, Quebec: Reader's Digest Association, 1995.

Sunset Western Garden Book. Menlo Park, California: Lane Publishing Co., 1994.

Index